MOUNTAINS, MADNESS, & *Miracles*

4,000 MILES ALONG THE APPALACHIAN TRAIL

MOUNTAINS, MADNESS, & *Miracles*

4,000 MILES ALONG THE APPALACHIAN TRAIL

LAURALEE BLISS
"Blissful"

WhiteFire
—— Publishing ——

*to Jackie & Mike
May you enjoy
the AT in a
wonderful wander!
Lauralee Bliss*

MOUNTAINS, MADNESS, & MIRACLES: 4,000 MILES
ALONG THE APPALACHIAN TRAIL

WhiteFire Publishing
13607 Bedford Rd NE
Cumberland, MD 21502

ISBNS: 978-1-939023-10-0 (print)
            978-1-939023-11-7 (digital)

*For all those in the midst of accomplishing their dream
or have yet to see their dream fulfilled...
I dedicate this book.*

"Remote for detachment, narrow for chosen company, winding for leisure, lonely for contemplation, it [the Appalachian Trail] beckons not merely north and south but upward to the body, mind and soul of man."

~ Myron Avery, *In the Maine Woods*, 1934

PART I

NORTHBOUND FROM GEORGIA TO MAINE
2007

CHAPTER ONE

I COULD DROP DEAD

JUNE, 2007
CARLISLE, PENNSYLVANIA

I stare at the physician in disbelief. I'd wanted a second opinion, one that would get me a pass out of this cold, antiseptic place called a hospital. Instead, a doctor is trying to give me an admission ticket.

"Are you kidding?" I say. "It's that serious?"

"We won't know until we run some more tests. You don't want to go back out hiking with no medical help around and then drop dead. It's better to find out. Heart conditions are more difficult to diagnose in women. We don't take any chances with chest pain."

Did he just say I could drop dead while hiking the trail? Fear washes over me. This doctor has to be joking. The Appalachian Trail is many things. It's steep, flat, winding, twisting, challenging mind, body, and soul. It can make knees ache and feet wish they were nestled in soft slippers rather than soggy trail runners. But now a doctor claims I could drop dead hiking it. It never occurred to me that I could actually die on this journey of mine.

"Well then, I guess I'd better find out if I'm okay," I tell him in a meek voice. I turn to the cold white wall, trying to blink back the tears. This isn't supposed to be happening. I'm forty-four years old and in the best shape of my life. I've lost twenty pounds and dropped two clothing sizes since starting this hiking trip back in March. As it is, my hiking pants would be falling down if not for the waist belt of my backpack that keeps them up. I know I'm not eating the right foods at times, but surely that shouldn't drive me to a hospital bed with an IV in my arm and a nurse trying to give me a nitroglycerin tablet for an unknown heart ailment.

Okay, God. There has to be a reason for this delay. Maybe I was being spared some further calamity from gripping me or my son on the trail. Or maybe this signaled the death of a dream. I would end my quest to hike the entire Appalachian Trail from Georgia to Maine at the halfway point within the bounds of a hospital in Carlisle, Pennsylvania. What the Pennsylvania rocks hadn't yet inflicted upon me my own excesses would—with doctors convinced that my chest pain signaled a major heart condition. Halfway along on my journey and it's come to a screeching halt.

I blame it on the half gallon challenge.

I grimace, thinking back on what my teenage son Joshua, or "Paul Bunyan"—his trail name—said. Just a few days ago we'd stopped at Pine Grove Furnace State Park in Pennsylvania, just north of the halfway point along the Appalachian Trail. At the general store, hikers indulge in a tradition called the Half Gallon Challenge, requiring one to consume a half gallon of ice cream to mark the halfway point on the trail. Paul Bunyan joked how someone had posted the phone numbers for the nearest rescue squad and hospital on the outside wall of the store, as if to warn all would-be challengers of the potential risks involved. We shrugged it off, laughing as we shared a half gallon carton of cookies and cream. I thought about my past gallbladder issues but pushed it aside. This was the midway victory lap, and I would enjoy this refreshing treat on a hot summer's day. But when I ate my last spoonful, I wondered if I would come to regret it.

A few nights later, I awoke to the worst pain. It started in my chest and radiated to my back. When I reported to the emergency room to have it looked at, I told the doctors it was likely my gallbladder raising a ruckus because of my excesses in the eating department. Instead they believe I'm having heart issues. They want to admit me for further testing.

I can't believe this. I'm actually being admitted to the hospital, right smack in the middle of my hike.

Once everything is ready, the nurse wheels me to a room in the medical ward. They hook me up to a telemetry unit that will monitor my heart. I stare out the window that overlooks a modest mountain range in the distance, the same mountain range I'm supposed to be crossing on the Appalachian Trail today. Instead of hiking, I'm in bed, wired up with electrodes, waiting for tests on the ol' ticker.

This isn't supposed to happen!

I face yet another challenge rendered by trail life. Another mountain to conquer. Another test of faith. Another moment that forces me to choose between peace or crippling anxiety.

Okay, God. My life is in Your hands. And so is my heart, in whatever shape it's in.

Yet the real test still remains. Can I accomplish this one dream that has stayed with me some thirty years? Can I hike the entire Appalachian Trail and do it with my only son? Is this really what I'm supposed to do, or is it sheer madness?

CHAPTER TWO

ONE LONG DREAM OR A NIGHTMARE?

1977 TO 2007

"Patience and diligence, like faith, remove mountains."

~ William Penn, Quaker

"There's no way I'm hiking again with you. Every time we go out, you have to race ahead. And then you say we can make time on these flat sections. I'm about ready to pass out!"

I'm not sure how to answer my sister. We're teens, out for a simple wander in the woods. But our simple three-mile jaunt to some picturesque waterfalls in Shenandoah National Park has turned into an eight-mile ordeal of rough canyon walking. And we only have one small can of juice between us. I swallow down any answer and just hike. Hopefully we will reach our destination soon before my sister gets really mad, or we both get really thirsty.

I can't help it, I love to hike. I love conquering a trail with speed and gusto while enjoying the beauty of creation that surrounds me. Trying to hike with me is like racing a sports car filled with high-octane gas. All I want to do is conquer this thing called a trail and make it my own. At the tender age of fourteen, I hear trails calling my name. They beg the questions: *Do you dare try to master me? Can you take what*

I have to offer, propelling you up some steep mountainside, through all kinds of terrain, to some far-off conclusion? As a young teen, and still rather ignorant, I answer with an unequivocal, "You bet I can. I'll take you on...anytime, anywhere."

Little do I realize I'm setting myself up for a thirty-year odyssey to conquer a special trail. The trail of trails. The Appalachian Trail. It runs from Georgia to Maine through fourteen states, numerous national forests, state and national parks, towns, farmlands, roads, and yes... mountains. Over 2,000 miles. I first learn of the trail from a park ranger in Shenandoah National Park who points out the famous footpath winding through the woods, marked by white rectangles painted on the trees. The white blaze is the symbol of a scenic footpath, not only traversing state to state and scenery to scenery, but in my case, from maddening dream to hopeful fulfillment.

Let me at you! my heart screams. *One day I will conquer you!* That is, when the timing is right. After all, I'm still in high school. Then comes four years of college and who knows what else. But I remain fascinated by the idea of hiking a trail of this magnitude. A wondrous journey presented to me at an impressionable age. Walking from state to state. Seeing all there is to see and by the power of my own two feet. Not by car, mini motor home, plane, train or anything else but crossing state lines using pure muscle power, transporting an eager soul from Georgia to Maine. What an adventure. What a goal.

What madness...for a young teen. Still, I buy a few books to learn what a trip like this will entail. I'll read about the adventure anyway, even if I can't yet live it. The title of the book I choose is enough to send goose bumps racing up my arms and a chill skittering down my back. *Appalachian Hiker: Adventure of a Lifetime.* It reeks of all I want to experience. The author, Edward Garvey, was one of the first to hike the entire trail and document it in a day-by-day series of events. I read the book cover to cover. I make it a yearly ritual to read it. I want to do what Ed Garvey did. I want to hike the entire Appalachian Trail.

In the months and years that follow, I search for ways to cross paths with it. I scan road maps to see if one of our family trips will intersect it. I look out the car window for any telltale sign of a white blaze, a metal trail marker, or just a wooden sign inscribed with the magical words, APPALACHIAN TRAIL. At a particular state park in Pennsylvania where the trail intersects, I beg my parents to hike a short section with me. They agree, along with snapping a picture of me beside an Appalachian Trail sign, my candy-cane-striped daypack slung over one shoulder. One small step for a teen. One giant step toward some future event yet to be written.

In the years that follow, I continue mentioning this peculiar dream of mine to parents, siblings, and friends, even if they think it's only a passing fascination. "Get serious," well-meaning mentors will admonish. And I do.

Even if others don't seem to understand it, you have to chase your destiny with determination. You're the one who can make your dream come true, if you believe in it and step out in it. No one is going to do it for you. And when you reach out in faith, God meets you. He met me in this madness I had concocted as a fourteen-year-old—the idea of hiking the entire Appalachian Trail. Though for a while it remains a seed hidden away in the cold ground, waiting to mature when the conditions are right.

* * * *

While the seed lies dormant, I pursue educational goals like graduating college with a degree in nursing. Not long after, I give my heart and my life to Christ and look to Him for my goals in life. Such as where I should practice nursing. Only one place comes to mind after scouring the nursing recruitment literature. The university hospital in Charlottesville, Virginia, which happens to lie in close proximity to Shenandoah National Park...and, you guessed it, the Appalachian Trail.

I interview and am offered a nursing job. I head to Virginia to make a new life. My days off are spent exploring the trails of Shenandoah, taking photos, and marveling in the beauty of God's creation. I settle into a church and meet my future husband, Steve. He ends up my perfect match, one who shares a similar love for the outdoors. But little does he know the dreamer he'd married or how he would be instrumental in making those dreams come true. He would become a major pillar holding up the house of dreams. How we need such pillars in people when we are called upon to do something extraordinary. To steady us when we're about to fall. To hold up our arms as men did with Moses. We do well to wait on the pillars God will bring into our life's journey. They help us live out the dream and make the impossible possible.

So it is with Steve. But first comes marriage. Then the baby carriage...the birth of our first and only child, Joshua. Parenthood, responsibilities, jobs. Moving to a new home. Settling into activities like homeschooling Joshua, keeping house, and the newest area that opens up for me—writing novels. But the other dream, that seed planted long ago, that dream of hiking a 2,000-mile-long trail, still lurks in the background. At times the desire rears its head as if to let me know the seed is still in existence. I continue reading books about the trail, like my well-used *Appalachian Hiker: Adventure of a Lifetime.* The seed is still there in some form despite a career and marriage, despite child-rearing and homeschooling, despite caring for the vegetable garden, roses, and the family dog. A dream of one day completing the entire Appalachian Trail.

Hiking began at a young age. Here, Paul Bunyan is only eight months old when we introduced him to his first Appalachian Trail shelter at Calf Mountain in Shenandoah National Park.

But it's all the tasks of life for now. Joshua's walking and talking. I grow weary of chasing our rambunctious coonhound who loves to roam the neighborhood. I clean the house and make nice meals. I'm trying to be that perfect mom and wife. But what about the seed of a long-distance hike? How I want to break open the tough outer hull to let a bit of nourishment reach the living matter. I want just a bit of growth, no matter how small. A morsel of faith injected into a dream so that the dream might take root.

I decide to mention my dream to Steve. "You know what I've been thinking?" Pause. "When Joshua is old enough, like sixteen, he and I are going to hike the Appalachian Trail together."

We gaze at our three-year-old son who gives us an impish grin before racing off with a toy in one hand and a blue blanket clutched in the other. Steve says nothing. I think he nods. Thirteen years is a long time. There's plenty of time for things to change and this idea to subside. For now it's just words. But words can have a tremendous impact on our lives. Words are also a confession of faith. On the outside, words seem to have no such power to move anything. But isn't that the essence of faith, to believe in something yet unseen? And just the nourishment needed to make a seed take root and grow, ever so slowly.

* * * * *

Years tick by. I continue to homeschool Joshua and write books. I'm still a dutiful wife and mom. But a part of me remains restless—the spirit of adventure aching to be released. I manage to calm a restless heart with some mini adventures, like a backpacking trip here and there. But as Joshua grows older and he begins to experience more of the outdoor life, I start to make plans for a long-distance hike on the Appalachian Trail. Only four years remain until Joshua turns sixteen. His schooling will be wrapping up. It seems the perfect time to go.

I step out and set a date for the hike of all hikes. March, 2007.

I don't say much to Steve about the date. Instead we try out a portion of the Appalachian Trail near our home. I don my backpack, overloaded with gear, and we set out to hike a difficult section in Virginia called the Three Ridges. On that hike I'm quickly thrust into the rigors of trail life I never knew existed. Ideas are one thing. Reality is another.

Every day it rains. I lay in my tent listening to the sound of a million raindrops from a violent thunderstorm when a light mist of condensation begins falling on me. Not only is it raining on the outside of the tent but on the inside, too. I decide to make a mad dash for the trailside shelter and better protection. I crawl out of my tent to discover a thousand earthworms have materialized from the ground and are now squirming their way toward me. I crawl back inside the tent and wail. How can I possibly do this maddening thing called the Appalachian Trail? Whatever possessed me to want to try? I'd read the books and fantasized for years. But really I know so little about what it means to live in the actual trenches of trail life, now rapidly filling with puddles, mud, and earthworms by the hundreds.

The next day we trudge through rugged terrain in the rain and fog. There are no views but plenty of blisters and pain. My pack feels like it weighs a hundred pounds. We come to another shelter to discover the occupants had moved out when they heard our family was coming. I'm grateful to have a dry place to spend the night, but I'm still discouraged about trying to do a long-distance hike. I don't think I can cope with the difficulties. The rain. The pain. The worms. And to make matters worse, I discover a mouse has nibbled away the nose pads to my glasses at the last trailside shelter. This really is madness.

But then I discover that one of the other occupants sharing the shelter that night had completed a hike of the entire Appalachian Trail. I confess to Animal (his trail name) my doubts that seem higher than any mountain we'd climbed that day.

He nods in an understanding way. "You have to realize, the trail is 90% mental. Most anyone can handle the physical aspects. It's the mental game you need to overcome. From what you've been saying, how you've wanted to do this since you were young, I believe you've got a good shot at accomplishing it."

Wow. It's like Animal was sent as a sign to keep my dream alive. Despite the hardship and the doubts, don't give up. Stay the course. And believe in what you feel you're supposed to do.

* * * * *

Time continues to melt away, and now two years remain before the big start day. In all that time, I've hardly talked to Steve about my plan. So one day I decide to broach the subject. I tell him how I would like to hike the whole trail with Joshua, starting the first of March, 2007. It will take us six months to accomplish it.

"You can't be gone that long!" he protests. "I think you should do it over several summers. Then I can join you."

I could do it that way, but that's not my heart's desire. I really want to do the whole trail in one year. But I know, too, I need help. To be gone for months on end, with the need for support, means I need my husband to agree to the plan.

But Steve is not in the agreeing mood.

And what about Joshua, my supposed co-hiker in this venture...?

JOSHUA

Yeah, I heard about this whole deal when I was fourteen years old. I really couldn't even think about it, to be honest. But when I do consider it, I wonder how I can do 2,000 miles and six months of hiking.

Then I start to get defensive when I'm told I have to go. "Mom, this is your dream," I tell her. "Why do I have to go, just to carry your stuff? Why do I want to take six months out of my life to hike?" For me, I like a weekend of hiking. But six months? And the idea of taking that much time away from friends? No way.

LAURALEE

Sigh. This is not working out. The family appears dead set against this. They have no vision to hike the trail like I do. I've had thirty years to nurture this dream. They've had less than two years to grab hold of the idea. Time is running out.

One day, Steve decides we ought to do some more hiking as a family. This time we'll do the Appalachian Trail through Shenandoah National Park near our home. I'm happy for anything to get our feet back on the trail, literally as well as figuratively. The more we hike, the more we'll know the ins and the outs of this thing, and the better chance that madness can turn into reality. Or at least a dream might take hold.

Off we go, tackling a few weekends of Appalachian Trail hiking through Shenandoah National Park. I'm nervous, I must admit. The second day on the trail we plan to hike thirteen miles. The most I've ever hiked in one day is ten miles, and that was a day hike. I didn't know if I could make it. But I do and end up with sore muscles and toenails ready to fall off. That night I'm in no mood to talk to any of the other hikers in residence inside the shelter. I'm hurting too much to enjoy any of this. Doubts plague me once again.

But now I start to realign my thinking. If I want this hike to succeed, something inside me needs to give. An attitude check of sorts. The next time we continue on our trek through Shenandoah, I plan to set a few things straight in my heart:

1.   I will have a better attitude, even if the hike proves difficult.
2.   I will be a friend of the trail. No matter how tired or grouchy I am, I will speak to other hikers and not fall into isolationism.
3.   I will do what I need to do, putting aside fleshly pain and fatigue to stand in faith.

J O S H U A

At this point in our hiking it's all nondescript to me. I'm okay about doing Shenandoah as long as I don't have to hike long days. In fact the next time we go out on the trail, we only hike two miles to our first spot for the night. That's more my style. We arrive at the shelter to see smoke from a fire. My heart falls, figuring there are tons of hikers. Instead there are two scruffy guys called Disney and Mailar. I get to talking to them and find out they are "thru hikers" doing the whole Appalachian Trail. Wow, people really do hike this whole thing. It's interesting to find out why they are doing it.

Later that evening I decide my job is to gather wood for the fire. At one point I find this thick log, five feet long. I try breaking it by throwing my weight against it, but it's not working.

Disney sees me struggling and shouts, "Hey Paul Bunyan, let me give you a hand with that."

We work together to break up the wood and bring it back to the shelter. I tell my mom what Disney called me, and she immediately says, "Hey, you have a trail name now! Paul Bunyan."

After the experience of earning my trail name, I feel like I fit in with the hiking crowd. Things are changing inside me. I still think I'm too young to do this, and the distance is too far. Maybe at age nineteen or twenty a person will hike over 2,000 miles. But at age sixteen, I'm leery about it all.

LAURALEE

So what should we do? Go for this mega hike or not?

Not long after our wander through Shenandoah National Park is complete, Steve comes to me with a thought or two. "You know, Lauralee...if you were to start the trail in March then I could join you in the summer. And if we can knock off the northern part of Virginia right now, that would put you farther along. I could then hike with you in New England, which is my favorite area."

I'm still on his first sentence. Did he just say, *If you were to start the trail in March...?*

He did! I had the blessing of my husband to do the trail!

Did I have to stress over it? Lose sleep? Argue with everyone to change minds and hearts? Not a bit. I rest in the knowledge that everything is under control. Not by my will but in allowing God to work in other people's hearts. He has this thirty-year-old dream all figured out, if I'm patient to wait and see what unfolds.

* * * * *

Besides my husband's approval, I also seek out the counsel of leaders and close friends. I believe there's wisdom found in a multitude of counselors, and I can always use wisdom, especially in an extreme venture such as this. First I talk to the pastor's wife about my plan. I'm not sure how it's going to be received. It's unusual, of course, to spend months hiking— until she mentions her own interest in one day climbing Kilimanjaro. What an interesting coincidence. Whenever we meet after that, she asks how plans are coming for the trail.

One Sunday in church she rushes up to me. "You must meet our guest today, Lauralee! She's hiked the whole Appalachian Trail!"

What? In our little church of 80 people, a visitor has come who has actually accomplished what I want to do? I can't wait to meet her. And I do, in the women's rest room of all places. She hiked the trail in 2005. Her trail name is Odyssa. She shares about what she did and what an adventure it was and encourages me to do it. Little do I realize that five years later, in 2011, this woman will become the world record holder for the fastest time hiking the Appalachian Trail. Jennifer Pharr Davis, i.e. Odyssa. Small world.

Another confirmation of my plans comes at a surprise birthday brunch that my friends throw for me. I'm close to the start of my dream journey—a mere two months away. My good friend had put some money in one of the cards, along with a note:

To buy what you need for your thing (meaning my hiking thing).

I'm touched. I open yet another gift, and it's a book entitled, *Live Like You Were Dying*. The friend who gave me the book knew nothing about my plan to hike for six months.

Wow.

I still have a few other important people left to ask, namely my book editors who have some pending writing projects for me to finish. Three books are due out that fall. But all of my editors are willing to work around my trail schedule and even express excitement for my plan.

Everything is falling into place. I have my husband on board. My son is interested. My book editors agree to work with my strange schedule. My friends give me messages in cards, Scripture verses, letters, e-mails, and gifts.

It certainly appears as if this dream of mine, born at age fourteen, is heading for fruition. But there is still much to do to get ready for a six-month hike. The lists are growing. The butterflies are fluttering. Time is growing nigh.

Will I be ready?

CHAPTER THREE

MEALS, MAIL DROPS, AND OTHER MADNESS

"The secret of success is to be ready when your opportunity comes."

~ Benjamin Disraeli, British Prime Minister

How does one prepare for something as monumental as hiking the Appalachian Trail for months on end? Many enjoy a weekend trip into the woods. Or camp and hike for a summer vacation. To take six months out of life to hike one trail, over 2,000 miles in length, is not a normal, everyday occurrence. But this is my calling. My dream. My reality that's fast approaching. And I need to get ready.

There are the necessities of life, naturally. Nutrition, water, shelter, clothing. There's the aspect of leaving loved ones behind, as well as work and home life. For me, there's also a need for spiritual preparedness. I never forgot Animal's advice that it's a mental journey more than a physical one. So the first order of business in any massive endeavor is for me to start praying and discovering what to do.

"A man's mind plans his way, but the Lord directs his steps and makes them sure" (Proverbs 16:9). It's good to have a glimpse at what those steps might be so the journey is successful. And my glimpses begin with some prayerful consultation with the One who knows things a lot better than

I do. Sure, it's hard to think that the God of the universe would even consider helping out a forty-four-year-old mother of a homeschooled teenager prepare for some trek in the woods. He must be more interested in the needier things in life. The things worthy of His undivided attention. The starving, the wars going on. The widow and the orphan. But this is THE God we are talking about, right? Who am I to limit His greatness? That He can guide the large and the small, even things that may seem a bit unusual, like me going on some long-distance adventure in the deep woods. Why not?

Next on the list, I decide to put my gift for organization to the test and use it in planning. Gear for the hike is one of the many issues I tackle. Researching gear choices. Chatting with fellow hikers online and in person. Everyone has their opinions on the matter. A synthetic sleeping bag versus one made of down. A smaller backpack versus the big clunker I've had for several years. Wearing boots versus trail runners. The amount and variety of clothing. Even the type of backpacking stove. Decisions, decisions, and none of them easy. This is truly madness of a different sort.

But there's one thing all hikers seem to agree on. The weight of the backpack you plan to carry. Since I must bear a loaded backpack with knees that aren't quite as young as they used to be, hauling it up and down steep mountains, weight is critical. I'm glad to have my son along for the journey, as we plan to split up carrying some of the gear like the tent with the poles, and the cooking supplies. For me, it's a challenge not to go overboard when it comes to clothing and life's necessities. Nothing is mapped out. Just like an infant who must learn to walk and eat table food, you get wiser as you gain trail miles. You learn what to do without and hopefully lighten the load.

Next on the agenda is nutrition. Coming from a German heritage, food is a big deal. When my father learns that I'm going on this lengthy trip, his immediate questions surround food choices. If I will have enough to eat. Naturally there must be resupply points on a six-month hike. Some hikers choose to buy food from stores along the way. Others mail themselves food in boxes called mail drops. We settle on a combination of the two—mailing the main bulk of foodstuffs to ourselves at various post offices or hostels along the way and buying whatever perishable provisions we will need (like bread and cheese).

In the following weeks, food prep for the mail drops begins in earnest. The food dehydrator works nonstop making beef jerky and drying canned chicken. Huge bags of frozen vegetables are reduced to tiny zippered snack bags of produce that weigh a fraction of an ounce. The kitchen counter rapidly fills with homemade snack bars and granola. I make G.O.R.P. bags by the dozens, trying to come up with creative combinations rather than just the simple, "Good Ol' Raisins and Peanuts." A scoop of this, a spoonful of that. I hope all this effort will help the hike succeed. I'm certainly working hard enough.

Our basement turns into a shipping office for our food drops to send along the trail. Boxes cover every square inch of the table. In those boxes the journey is laid out before me, and it's a scary prospect. I fear the outcome. Will I succeed or will I fail? Will I reach each of those boxes along the journey? Or will my effort be wasted along with the money spent to prepare and mail them? At this stage I only want to hear God's voice in my heart, work through the simple things, and take it one step at a time. These are lessons I'll learn sooner rather than later as the adventure unfolds.

There are also the leftover tasks in my writing and at home that I need to wrap up. The magnitude of the journey swiftly hits me one day as I gaze at my surroundings. There are items, for instance, that I won't need for six months. My home is changing from an 1800-square-foot ranch-style home to a 4,000-cubic-inch backpack holding a few meager belongings. My shelter each night will be a tent, a wooden shelter, or a hostel in a strange town. My nice bed with its comfortable pillow topper will be reduced to a sleeping pad and sleeping bag. My closet is a nylon bag stuffed with a few hiking clothes. You don't consider all this until it's suddenly thrust upon you. I've experienced some weekend backpacking but nothing to this scale. I will turn into a true wanderer with no house, no furniture, a few meager possessions, and the inability to control what lies before me. A scary prospect.

Besides my own preparedness, I have another person to consider in the equation. My sixteen-year-old son. I would love it if he were to come on board with his own ideas about what to bring, what changes he must make, etc. After all, he needs to get ready, too...

JOSHUA

Right. I look at some of the gear to see what I might need, but I think, *Hey, my parents got it under control.* Mom will get the stuff together. But there are some things I do want to put in my backpack, like a small chess set, a deck of cards, and a book to read. And of course, my two-pound knife. When I did the other backpacking trips through Shenandoah, I always brought this huge sheath knife. It's symbolic.

As far as getting into shape, I figure that's what the trail is for. Mom did a lot of running and walking to help get ready, but I'm not worried. To be honest, I still don't think we're going to do this trip. I think once we get to Georgia and start the trail, we'll hike a few days, say, "That's nice, we saw the start," turn around and go home. So why worry about all the planning?

That's what he thinks! I'm in this thing for the long haul, and I plan for Joshua's gear right along with mine. I did begin the physical preparation for this dream several years before by engaging in a running program. It progressed well until I severely sprained my ankle in 2004, setting me back nearly two years. I dearly wanted to get back on my feet, not just in running but ultimately hiking. But I struggled with ongoing tendonitis and sought out a sports doctor for suggestions.

"Well," he said, "you might have to consider that you won't be able do the things you once did. Like hiking. For instance, I can no longer pitch because of a shoulder injury, and I love baseball."

I remember looking at the baseball mementos on the wall of the exam room. *You mean to say, I'll never hike again?*

I refused to accept his prognosis. That couldn't be my lot in life, not after years of nurturing a dream. In desperation I switched doctors and found one that believed in my goals. He put me in touch with a good physical therapist, and through patience and extensive rehabilitation, I was able to hike again.

The final year before the hike, I walked many miles to get muscle groups in shape. On occasion I loaded up a backpack and toted it around the neighborhood, drawing curious looks from the neighbors in the process. I hiked the roads, some of which overlook the majestic Blue Ridge Mountains and the Appalachian Trail while wondering if I would accomplish this hike.

What better testing of faith than to bring oneself to a place of need? You can train as best you can. Prepare for the physical parts and gather your gear. But trust is where it's all at. When we look at life, we are constantly in a place where faith is being tested. It can be in the simplest of things, like believing the car keys will be found in a logical place, if you're running late. Or faith in monumental things, like the money needed to pay the bills or what to do when your only car has a bad transmission. Even faith in suffering, such as what I endured with my ankle injury, yet believing I would hike again despite the prognosis.

Now the greatest test of faith up until this point has arrived. I will abandon all I know for the unknown, forcing me to draw on strength and wisdom through Scripture, prayer, words offered by others, and simply walking a lonely trail. On the journey I plan to carry a small New Testament and Psalms. But I also carry with me words of encouragement and inspiration given to me by friends and family. One such message, written by my good friend Sherry, stays close to my heart even to this day:

> *I won't tell you to "Go with God"*
> *For God will go with you*
> *His word will be a lamp unto your feet*
> *And a light unto your path.*
> *He'll hear your prayer before it's uttered*
> *His strength will be your supply*
> *His presence will be your abiding joy*
> *Your help in time of need.*
> *The prayers of the saints will hold you up,*
> *In times of trial and pain*
> *So don't fight your battles alone*
> *And you can run the race to win.*
> *With a message in your heart to share*
> *With those you meet long the way,*
> *We'll pray for God's divine encounters*
> *So that His truth may enter their hearts.*
> *And when you come to the end of your trail,*
> *And look to heaven with tears of joy in your eyes*
> *Grounded more in His love and faithfulness,*
> *You'll say, "Look what God has wrought!"*

I keep the words of encouragement as a reminder of faithfulness. I cling to such words for the journey ahead. I'm not fooling myself. This will be the hardest thing I have ever done.

Ready as I'll ever be.

I hope.

CHAPTER FOUR

WILL I MAKE IT PAST DAY ONE?

GEORGIA

"Today is the first day of the rest of your life."

~ Charles E. Dederich, Synanon founder

The backpacks are packed. The food drops are taped up for the first part of the journey. The dog is in good hands until Steve returns. Everything is ready for our departure to Georgia and Amicalola Falls State Park where we will begin the hike. We're ready to start my thirty-year dream to hike the Appalachian Trail.

But then Paul Bunyan spikes a temperature.

I develop a nasty sore throat.

Dark clouds drape across the sky, promising a deluge.

Uh, oh.

We will not be driving down on February 28 to begin my thirty-year odyssey. I will not plant my feet on the trail March 1 as expected. We're too sick to go.

I fuss. Cry a little. The proverbial questioning begins. The answer to *why?* If I did not hold on to the Scripture that a man plans his way but the Lord directs his steps, I do now. It's the only thing I can grasp. Still, saddlebags filled with doubt drag down my faith while questions take the spotlight. Am I really supposed to do this hike? Or is the rug being pulled out from underneath me, tripping me so I don't go through with this outlandish scheme of mine?

Actually, there's a lesson to be learned. Like adjusting to changing circumstances. Everything you once knew is tossed to the wind of adventure. The sooner I accept that fact, the better. And it's a good thing, because on a long-distance hike, there is no such thing as status quo. You don't know what each day will bring. It's useless to plan for it. You really have to go with the flow.

Since my departure date has changed, so has everything else. We rescue our dog from the kennel. I alter the dates on the mail drops to be sent out. Steve grows anxious as he'd planned to be out only ten days with us at the start of the hike. Now his time on the trail is slowly dwindling. The frustration is palpable, but there's little we can do. I embrace a new beatitude of life when trials begin. *Blessed are the flexible, for they will find joy and peace as they wait upon that perfect timing.* Sounds like a good one.

While my son and I recuperate from our maladies, and I cope with the changing plans, I watch the weather unfolding in Georgia. During our convalescence, seven inches of rain falls, drenching the very ground we were to tread. My questioning subsides as I read accounts of rivers overflowing their banks and people contending with flash flooding. Maybe God does know what He's doing. He didn't make us ill, of course, but He can use trials to shape the trail. If we had left on our original start date of March 1, it would have been a wet, sloppy, muddy, discouraging way to begin six months of trail life.

Several more days come and go as we remain stuck on the tarmac of sickness. Paul Bunyan continues to falter in the eating department as he battles his cold. I've taken to cradling a box of tissues. The weather clears with bright blue skies, but we are still in Virginia. Ever the optimist—or trying to be—I make an alternate plan. If possible, our new plan is to leave March 4 for Georgia and be on the trail March 5. Just having some plan of action makes my sinuses clear and strikes a spark of joy and anticipation. If no other catastrophe bars our way, we might actually make it to the starting point of this hike.

Early on the morning of March 4 I look around my home for the last time. I won't be returning to this place until sometime in mid-May when I will have walked 900 miles to get here. I'm abandoning my castle, my call as keeper of the home, for a new home in the woods. It's unnerving, leaving a place of security for the unknown. I can understand a bit what missionaries and the military must undergo in their psyche. All security and comfort is thrown to the wind for an unknown situation. It really is akin to stepping off a cliff and letting oneself be caught up in the wind of faith. When I finally close and lock the front door, I am saying farewell to my prior existence and hello to a life I know so little about. *God, help me.*

After a ten-hour drive to northern Georgia, I catch my first glimpse of the mountain range we will traverse for the first week of the hike. It doesn't look much different from the mountains of Virginia. I feel somewhat better. We have survived our first major test with illness. The hike should be smooth sailing, at least for a little while.

Sleep is hard to come by that night in the motel room. I ought to be relishing the comfort of sheets, a blanket, and a nice soft mattress that will soon to be traded for the hard ground and a cramped sleeping bag. But my mind buzzes with the events of tomorrow—the ultimate adventure, our hike to the start of the Appalachian Trail atop Springer Mountain and what lies ahead.

We're up early the next day, greeted by clear skies and crisp weather. The butterflies are already making their rounds in my stomach. I want to feel the excitement, but I'm also filled with a fear of the unknown.

We drive to Amicalola Falls State Park and proceed to the visitor center where hikers register for their hike. Inside the visitor center, a petite woman is looking over some nature exhibits while a man is asking questions of the ranger. I take little notice of them as I make final preparations—like filling up my water container, using the modern restroom facilities one last time, putting tape on my foot, and savoring my last taste of civilization for a while.

Steve, Joshua, and I exit out the rear of the visitor center to see a large stone arch heralding the start of the Approach Trail. This path leads hikers over eight miles to Springer Mountain and the official start of the Appalachian Trail. I hope there will be someone around to take our picture. Lo and behold, the same couple we saw at the visitor center appears. The husband, we find out, is also starting his hike today. We exchange introductions. His trail name is Dr. B, a real physician on his second attempt to hike the entire trail. His wife is very glad that her husband has found like-minded people undertaking the ultimate trail adventure. We take one another's picture under the arch and then gaze at the mileage sign. The beginning of the Appalachian Trail still looms over eight miles distant, and from there, another 2,175 some odd miles to the final destination of Katahdin in Maine. But who can ponder such a far-off destination at a time like this? For me, I just want to accomplish today's task, reaching the summit of Springer Mountain.

I shoulder my pack that seems to be gaining weight the longer I stand there. I take up my hiking poles, whisper a prayer, and begin the Approach Trail. Steve and I walk but a half mile when Paul Bunyan falls behind. Calling to him around a bend in the trail, he ignores our plea to catch up and hike as a family. He claims he will take this at his own pace, if at all. I try not to let doubt creep in, even as I struggle with sudden pains erupting out of nowhere in my foot and knee. It appears everything is in rebellion.

Dread washes over me. What was I thinking? How can I possibly do some trail from Georgia to Maine? All the plans, the preparations, the dreams, are about to come crashing down in defeat on day one—before I even arrive at the official start of the Appalachian Trail on Springer Mountain.

We complete the mile up the Approach Trail to the top of Amicalola Falls. There I take off my pack and struggle with the feeling that I'm making the worst mistake of my life. I can hear it now when we arrive home in defeat. The sympathetic looks mixed with *I thought it would be too much.* Or other sentiments meant to comfort but act as barbs instead.

I turn to see Paul Bunyan stumbling up the trail. He throws down his pack in an act of surrender. I can tell from his face what he's thinking, and it's not looking good...

JOSHUA

You got that right. And this is what I'm thinking. *I'm not going any farther on this stupid thing. Man, I can't believe how steep it is. I'm not cut out for this. This is a joke. Maybe if I lag behind, we'll stop and rethink this plan.*

At this point I'm still wondering what's going on and what we're doing. It all seems weird to me. Maybe we'll get to the top of the mountain and say, *Okay, let's go back down and maybe head out again tomorrow and see what happens.* This will only be a one or two night thing. It can't go on for weeks. No way.

LAURALEE

Sigh. It looks like we may be turning around here at the restroom, atop the waterfalls that give the park its name.

One mile into the Approach Trail and we are throwing in the towel, before we even see the first white blaze. The unthinkable is about to happen. We are going to head home in utter defeat. *Oh God, how can this be?*

Suddenly a man clutching a cigarette appears from around the restroom, his head wrapped in a bandanna. He introduces himself as Flint. I immediately recognize the name from a hiking website on the Internet. His wife contacted me a few days before via the site where I'm keeping my online trail journal. She mentioned her husband's plan to start March 5 and that his name is Flint. I already have a connection to the trail!

The next moment we're joined by Dr. B, the man we met at the arch where we exchanged pictures. We all begin talking about the hike...and then we begin hiking together. I don't think any more about giving up or that Paul Bunyan lags behind. We're officially part of a hiking circle that will become the mainstay of long-distance hiking—a league of fellow adventurers who hold to some wild, farfetched dream of hiking the entire Appalachian Trail.

Not long into the hike I realize the value of that inner circle. When we come to a trail intersection, Dr. B and Flint wait patiently for Paul Bunyan to catch up. They refuse to leave him behind but acknowledge him as a vital member of the group. They take their time, enjoying a slow, relaxed pace on a fine spring day. And with that patience, Paul Bunyan seems to have more energy.

The doubts are taking flight. We are not going home after all. We are on our way north.

I continue to enjoy the picture perfect day with views garnered through leafless trees. In the distance I can see the summit of Springer rising up before me. Before reaching it, I wait for my husband to lead us there. It's a ritual I insist upon on our various hikes, that Steve, as the head of the pack and our home, lead his family to the conclusion of a day's

*Blissful, Paul Bunyan, and Steve begin their northbound
trek on Springer Mountain in Georgia*

wander. And he does as we all summit Springer Mountain, the southern terminus of the Appalachian Trail.

There's plenty of celebration and satisfaction at the accomplishment of this first goal. We take pictures of one another. Flint calls his wife on his cell phone to inform her that our ragtag group has arrived. I stare at the plaque of the hiker embedded on the rock and then at the first painted white blaze of the trail that will begin a series of blazes covering a distance of over 2,000 miles. These white blazes will be my pied piper in a way. I will follow them all the way to the end. Except that trying to imagine going the distance to Maine is too fantastic to ponder. It might as well be some planet in a far-off galaxy. I can only think of this journey one day at a time. And right now, exhausted by the long hike and the emotional rollercoaster I've been riding, I'm just glad to be at the summit.

We lug our gear over to the shelter area atop the mountain, aptly named the Springer Mountain Shelter. To my dismay, a multitude of tents are set up. A reunion is in full progress. A bunch of hikers who hiked the trail last year have gathered to swap stories and, I'm guessing, meet the baby-faced newbies of this year's trail class. I am an infant hiker nursing a farfetched dream, with no idea what kind of adventure awaits me. I do know one thing: I want to succeed and show these mature hikers lurking around the fire pit that I have what it takes to do this thing, as impossible as it may look.

Thus begins my first night on the trail. No sooner do I settle in my sleeping bag when the wind begins to howl. We'd heard stories of the high winds atop Springer Mountain, but I took the warning with a grain of salt. Until the tent fabric rattles like a paper bag when the stakes are yanked out of ground. I switch on my headlamp and struggle out of the narrow, coffin-like tent to pound the stakes back into the stubborn ground. A few more times of keeping my tent upright in forty-mile-an-hour winds make for a sleepless night.

The next morning I fumble for my eyeglasses to put them on and find them missing from their case. Strange. I lift up my sleeping pad and resting there are the frames without the lenses. Agh! Panic attack! I can only surmise that in my nightmarish delirium of having to resurrect my tent multiple times during the night, I must have fallen asleep with my glasses on. Fear washes over me. I'm as nearsighted as one can be. Without glasses, I can't see. If I can't see, I can't hike. If I can't hike, that's the end of this trip.

A quick survey of the tent finally produces the lenses. I feverishly work to try and slip the lenses back into place, all the while praying the plastic banding on the frames doesn't break. Finally getting the lenses into some kind of position, I put on the glasses, only to find my vision totally distorted. It's obvious the lenses are not in correctly, but I dare not try to reposition them. If the band that holds the lenses breaks, I'll have no glasses and no way to hike the trail.

I inform Steve of my woes that morning, but it's me who

must adapt to this new situation until we can make it to a road crossing and a town where the glasses can be repaired. I now take on a new challenge—hiking without the ability to focus on where I'm going. I think about the blind man, Bill Irwin, who once hiked the trail with his guide dog back in 1990. Not that I'm blind, but with the rocks and roots distorted in my line of vision, it's affecting my gait. I have no choice but to ask God for help so I don't fall and injure myself.

Everyone is having a tough go of it that second day hiking and our first official day on the Appalachian Trail. The guys grunt and groan as we scale several peaks, including the steep Sassafras Mountain. By the time we reach a safe haven to find a campsite, darkness is quickly falling. We're all beat.

The next day Dr. B and Flint emphatically state they are not hiking any more long miles. They plan to head for the nearest road crossing and a hostel for the night. I'm all for the idea. Then we can go into the town of Dahlonega and find a vision center to repair my glasses.

The morning goes by quickly. Soon we're at the road crossing where we are picked up by the owner of the hostel. In a matter of an hour I'm at the vision center, expecting the optician to fix my glasses.

"I'm sorry," the girl at the counter says, "but without your prescription, we can do nothing."

My prescription! Oh, no. I never thought for a moment I would need my vision prescription. Frantically I try to reach my eye doctor, only to discover that today is his day off. If multiple things can go wrong, they are. This is starting to get scary. I knew there would be challenges on this hike, but to have this many trials so soon on the trail, it leaves me wondering what else can go wrong over the course of six months and some 2,000 miles?

I find out early in this game that trials show what an awesome God exists in this universe. I return the next morning to the vision center to find that my eye doctor has already faxed the prescription. When the optician finally looks at the glasses, she's amazed that I was even able to hike for two days. I put the lenses in backward and upside down. A miracle—of both the will and the vision necessary to carry on this hike. It must be that this trail is satisfying some purpose yet to be totally understood. Nothing so far on this venture has told me to stop, give up, or return to sender—that is, return to my native Virginia. It's only saying, *Press on, no matter what happens. Keep going.*

Okay...in modest trepidation.

* * * * *

After a few more days of hiking, Steve now must leave the trail and return to work. We've arrived in Hiawassee and the place where he's getting off the trail for good. With a heavy heart I say good-bye to my hero-husband. He's hiked with us, shuttled us via the van, given all us hikers a great hiker feed of hotdogs and sausages at Hogpen Gap, and even went off the trail to drive back to an outfitter and get my broken tent pole mended. (Yes, yet another mishap suffered early on the trail.) He asked a few hikers we had met—White Crow, Flint, Dr. B, and 357 Magnum—if they would watch over his family. Now the time of separation has come.

At the trailhead, I want to linger, to keep the good-byes going for as long as possible. I have such a lump in my throat, I can barely swallow. Tears well up in Steve's eyes too. I'm not certain when we'll see each other again. The emotion grows, but the trail, blazed in white, beckons to me. I shrug on my pack and force myself to turn away. Before Steve steers the van onto the road for the trip home, I catch a final glimpse of his face and think, *Until we meet again.*

Paul Bunyan and I are on our own.

CHAPTER FIVE

I QUIT!

THE STECOAHS &
GREAT SMOKY MOUNTAIN NATIONAL PARK

"Never, never, never, never give up."

~ Winston Churchill

When one makes the decision to hike a trail for a long period of time, the technology of this age is left behind for a simplistic lifestyle, or so one hopes. There are no laptops, iPads, televisions, etc. In 2007 when we began our northbound journey, smart phones were just entering the technological scene. We carry a few small gadgets with us—simple things, really, when compared to the modern conveniences available today. Paul Bunyan uses a voice recorder so he can record journal messages. I have a tiny MP3 player that runs on a single AAA battery (hence, no cumbersome charger to worry over). We do have a simple cell phone. But little else compared to one's house filled with all the products of easy living. Yet in the days that follow, I will find out how important one tiny gadget will become as I journey along the trail. How it will assist me in actually hiking it, as strange as that may seem.

During the next two weeks on the trail we accomplish a

few lofty goals but also meet with some challenges. We cross the first state line into North Carolina, marked by a gnarled oak tree with a bold, white blaze painted on the tree trunk. Known as Bly Gap, it's a proud symbol for all those struggling to make their way north. But I will not mention what looms ahead. North Carolina greets us with pointy mountain peaks that will be the symbol of a meandering trail that offers the unsuspecting hiker little sympathy.

We complete our first sixteen-mile day to hoof it into our first real trail town of Franklin, and just before the rains hit. A lonely Steve drives seven hours to Franklin for an unexpected family reunion. We endure our first real cold snap of the trail with daytime temperatures plummeting into the teens and a blustery wind that freezes our faces and makes lungs ache. I suffer my first fall of the trail, slipping on what I thought was a beautiful display of hoarfrost, only to discover that when the ice crystals melt, the trail turns into a slippery slope. I strain my right thigh muscle and have to baby it for a few days. But we also ascend several balds to views that offer a sneak peek of the Great Smoky Mountains gracing the distant horizon.

Ah, the Smokies. I have heard the horror tales concerning the park—like aggressive bears that make off with your food, challenging terrain, winter snows that can bury you in drifts, temperatures that make you wish you were back home, and little in the way of resupply. I fear and dread the Great Smokies. I think it will be the ultimate test of fortitude and strength. And it is, in a way I never thought it would be.

But first the Appalachian Trail brings us to the Nantahala River and the NOC or Nantahala Outdoor Center. Its primary function is rafting adventures on the river. Many hikers stop here for a stay, but we make the decision to pick up our mail drop of food and press on. It's interesting to take out our nylon stuff sacks and parcel out the food mailed to us. The park bench overlooking the river fills with zipper bags and food, coupled with the genuine frenzy of trying to figure out how much of the food we need to haul up and over the next few peaks. Passersby give us strange looks as we sit there amid all the plastic bags and the sorting. I wish I didn't feel so new at this game. True I've been hiking a few weeks. I just wonder when the strangeness will wear off so I'm no longer entertaining the nagging feeling that I'm not supposed to be out here. *Why are you here, in a remote wilderness, with your son, of all the places on earth?* Good question.

We hoist up heavy packs and begin the trek up toward Cheoah Bald, seven miles north. A scan of the elevation profile on the map shows what hikers face leaving the Nantahala River Gorge—an unforgiving, relentless climb. After five miles uphill we stop at the shelter for the night. Here we're introduced to a whole new string of would-be northbound hikers hoping to trek the entire length of trail. In residence are hikers with trail names like The Goats (who are actually three young women), Sniper, Freight Train, Stash, and Remix, among others. Little did we know but this group will also be the same hikers we encounter in the week ahead in the Smokies—all twenty years younger than me and full of youthful exuberance.

I can't help feeling strange, crowded together with young people in some shelter in the middle of nowhere. I feel like the old fuddy-duddy jammed in with the kids. I wonder if they think someone like me can't possibly make it to Maine. Or that I ought to be home where I belong. Confidence waxes and wanes out here in the middle of nowhere.

Before we enter the Great Smoky Mountains, there's a little section of trail about thirty miles in length called the Stecoahs. In words it doesn't sound like much. In actuality it's a series of relentless ups and downs. North Carolina likes to hurl a bit of cruel reality to the unsuspecting hiker. I discovered this when I first crossed the state line at Bly Gap and faced a test of pointed peaks. There are no short cuts to be had. No roundabout routes that take out steep sections that test limb and nerve. It's the gift the Stecoahs give us, wrapped up in a big red bow labeled *mental challenge.*

Now I watch as the two hikers ahead of me climb the next peak. And climb. And climb some more. Eventually I see them at the very pinnacle of some mountainous nose or summit looming before me. The steepness is not a pretty sight. I huff and puff, limping along as my knee begins to act up. I sit to put on a simple brace, hoping it will calm down. When I finally reach the "nose" of the mountain summit, the trail forms a long ski slope, descending straight down the other side before beginning another brutal climb up and over another mountainous pinnacle. Up and down, up and down. In hiking circles, these irritating climbs become known as PUDs or pointless ups and downs.

I call them tricksters of the mind. I begin to waver, not just in my tired joints but also in my psyche. I'm encountering the mental game I was warned about long ago before this hike began. Yes, there are physical challenges to be had. But like Animal once counseled me in a trailside shelter in Virginia, one must conquer the ultimate challenge. The battle of the mind that is 90% of this hike. Today I believe him. I'm facing mental challenges and utter mental fatigue, and it's weighing me down.

I stop on the trail. My knee aches as well as the thigh I'd previously injured. I think of the Smokies looming before me, less than two days away. An onslaught of doubt follows like a battery of missiles, hoping to break apart the wall of faith that's been building for some time. Next is the ugly parade of thoughts. *You'll never make it through the Smokies. There's no hope. You'll have to quit here. And everyone will say they told you so. Who said you could ever accomplish such a thing at your age?*

My faith is crumbling, and I'm not sure what to do. By this time Paul Bunyan has caught up to me. He can see by my face that something isn't right and asks what's wrong. I tell him I don't want to go on. I'm tired of these PUDs and this trail I've been hiking, even if it's been a mere two weeks. We reluctantly continue hiking, but my complaints are real. He suggests we stop short of our destination and camp somewhere. I don't even know if I can make it that far, in all honesty.

Then one of our little electronic gadgets comes to mind. The cell phone. I ask Paul Bunyan to dig it out while I mentally make a deal. *I need to know if I'm supposed to go on with this hike or stop. Whatever Steve suggests, I'll do.*

Cell coverage can be spotty in the mountains, but I connect with Steve and confess my woes. The fatigue. The multitude of aches and pains. And the real concern of making it through the Smokies. He comes back with gentle words of prayer and encouragement that infuse me with strength, watering dry and weary places, acting as an oil to soothe achy joints and refresh doubtful areas. He doesn't tell me to quit either, but he prays that everything will be okay so I can go on.

After that I'm able to pick up my pack and hike. Someone is holding up my trail arms like they did Moses, or in this case, my trail legs. I decide not to fret about goals or plans. Instead I will make every step count in the trek, whether many or few. Every moment on the trail means something. I'm not taking a step backward but a step forward. I think I understand even better why the astronauts made a big deal about one small step for man, one giant leap for mankind. On this trail, one step forward is a huge accomplishment. It means you haven't quit. You're still in the GaMe mindset, heading from Georgia to the monumental goal of Maine. One giant leap indeed, for the essence of a dream, even if it's just small steps.

The next day we're at the door of the Great Smoky Mountains. They are a beautiful but awesome sight, flanking the manmade Fontana Dam and lake. I can see the goal for the next day's crawl up the mountainside, a tiny fire tower perched atop Shuckstack Mountain. But that's for tomorrow. Today we head for a night's rest at a place called the Hike Inn and treat ourselves to a room along with a journey into town to feast on Mexican food.

We have no scheduled resupply until after we leave the Smokies, so packs are heavily laden with food. Neither one of us wants to put on our overloaded packs and cross the dam into the Smokies. But this is the next leg and the weather outlook is good, so off we go.

As I struggle toward Shuckstack Mountain and lunch at the fire tower, my knee is again acting up. I opt once more for the knee brace, something I don't like to use if I can help it. Pausing at a trail junction, I meet a college-aged daughter and her father also hiking the whole trail. The father takes one look at my pack, shakes his head and says, "That pack is way too big for the trail. You'll never make it carrying that." I manage a small smile and struggle on, trying hard not to think about what he just said. I could stand a little encouragement at this point, but on a lonely trail such as this, encouraging words sometimes are few and far between. Except for the calls I've made to Steve and the suggestions made by Paul Bunyan, any other encouragement I seek has to come from another source.

Like God. He can satisfy my need for encouragement. Relying on others sometimes brings disappointment, especially when they fail to come to the rescue. To expect others to understand is unrealistic. But God knows what I'm going through, whether it's a lonely trail or some other challenge in life. And He will be with me every step of the way.

Fear not [there is nothing to fear], for I am with you; do not look around you in terror and be dismayed, for I am your God. I will strengthen and harden you to difficulties, yes, I will help you (Isaiah 41:10a).

Sounds good to me. But struggling through the Great Smoky Mountains, the spells of discouragement seem to be knocking on the door of my psyche. At the junction to Shuckstack Mountain, I see another older woman resting there, her big backpack beside her. There are not many women my age hiking the trail. The majority of them are home where they belong, I suppose, holding down a job, caring for the kids, etc. We share a word of greeting before she moves on. For some reason, I'm too preoccupied to be overfriendly. I guess I'm ready for the view on Shuckstack that I've struggled and panted hard after to see.

Ditching my pack, I climb the rickety fire tower where the entire Stecoah Range lies before me—those series of nasty PUDs I'd gone up and over and down. But the view itself is still spectacular. I'm really in the Smoky Mountains. The tower sways in the wind as if nodding in agreement.

The next day, unexpected warm weather descends on the Smokies. The temperature soars into the 70s—unheard of in this normally blustery, cold, frozen land of the southern Appalachians. I find my body and soul rebelling, as if I'm allergic to this early call of summer. Spring fever affects my system in a strange way. I feel tired, worn out, and unenthused about the journey. Young people in their shorts and tops are lying out on rocks, soaking in the warmth. I, on the other hand, struggle with my too-huge pack (the guy on the trail told me I'd never make it anyway) and an empty stomach to boot. Earlier Paul Bunyan had forgotten our meeting place for lunch, and I've had nothing to eat for most of the day. Between the warm weather and the lack of energy, I begin to question my reasoning for being out here. This trail is slowly beating my flesh to a pulp, buffeting me to the point that I'm uncertain I want to go on.

Now I seriously consider the idea of quitting. It's not just a passing thought either, but a strong urge rising up within me. *I don't really have a reason to go on with this hike.*

I'm as old and worn out as I feel. No one thinks I can do it anyway. Why disappoint them?

When I arrive at the shelter for the night, all the twenty-something hikers are there enjoying themselves. Some are sunbathing on their sleeping pads. Others are laughing. They have music going on a small, hand-crank radio. The whole college scene displayed before me is like pouring lemon juice on a wound. I can't relate to their youthfulness, and no one can relate to me or how I feel. No one understands my struggles. The gas tank has run dry. I have no choice. If God chooses to let me alone, empty in my quest, there will be no energy or spirit left to propel me forward. This middle-aged hiker will have to go home. No doubt about it.

That evening I sit inside the shelter looking at the trail register. Many hikers leave entries in shelter registers to tell of their journeys. The registers are simply notebooks that become like diaries and a way to stay in communication with fellow hikers ahead or behind you. Of course I plan to leave my message with words certain to reflect how I feel inside. Like, *Guess it's time to go home* or something to that effect.

I look around and suddenly there's another hiker in the shelter with me. It's the same woman I'd seen the other day by Shuckstack Mountain. She's busy setting up her bedding. We exchange a few pleasantries. For some reason, I decide to open up to her about my weariness and my thoughts of leaving the trail.

"If you're thinking of quitting, this is what I was told," she says in this cute southern twang that I find refreshing. "Never quit on a rainy day, 'cause the sun will come out and you might think differently. If you're gonna quit, give it three days. Never quit when you're tired or it's the end of the day neither."

Little does she know, but her words are like sugar in my veins. They fill me with perseverance and the energy to go on. We talk some more. Her trail name is Hikernutt. When I find out she's but a year younger than me, it suddenly dawns on me that God had heard my despair. The funny thing is, the answer had been sitting right under my nose! Here's a woman my age, who understands the toils of hiking, who has her own mental and physical struggles. She wears two knee braces when she hikes but possesses a fierce determination to succeed. I have someone to confide in, even as I hear the college crew laughing and carrying on around the campfire that night. I have a hiking buddy. She's my answer to help me keep going.

A dear friend Hikernutt helped Blissful get through the Great Smokies

The next day is full of excitement. The weather is picture perfect with another unseasonably mild day to climb Clingman's Dome, the tallest peak in the Great Smoky Mountains National Park and the highest point on the Appalachian Trail. Stopping at Double Springs Gap Shelter for lunch, Hikernutt shares her food treats with me. She's like having my own trail angel on the journey. We're soon joined by the young hiker kids and lunch becomes a family affair. The youthful ones I found so irritating yesterday are now hiking companions today. We talk about the hike to

Clingman's Dome with the anticipation of seeing new terrain and mastering another climb.

The scenery quickly changes from brushy vegetation and balds to spruce-laden mountains with an earthy aroma that renews a weary soul. The trail meanders easily to the summit and a stone observation platform. Once there we take off our packs to enjoy a beautiful vista and take pictures of one another. Standing there on the highest point, clad in my shorts and T-shirt in mid-March, I can't help but be thankful for the great weather and great companionship. What a difference a day can make!

I'm feeling better and better about the trail in the Smokies as we meander along a narrow ridgeline, experiencing more breathtaking scenery. Arriving at dusk at our next destination for the night, I'm exhausted but happy as Hikernutt sets up her tent beside mine. I have my hiking pal, my teammate, a kindred spirit. To go Lone Ranger in this life of ours makes us vulnerable to the very enemies that seek to weigh us down and ultimately destroy our walk. It's never as clear as it is now on this journey.

I'm hiking a trail, yes, but I am also on a spiritual journey. A journey where every day I see spiritual principles being played out like never before. And on this particular section of the trail, I witness brotherly (or in this case sisterly) love come to light. Of bearing one another's burdens. Of encouraging one another when the walking gets rough. Even if your walk right now is simply going to your job or taking care of the kids, it's still a life's journey. Along the way there will be helpers to talk with and give you times of refreshment, to laugh with and even sing a little. I laugh with Hikernutt as we discuss our families, our dreams, our goals, along with the usual hiker talk of the next section of trail, the next equipment issue, the next good meal. Good conversation and companionship can go a long way.

JOSHUA

On the trail I found out quickly how friends can come and go. That's the thing with the trail—people can speed up, fall behind, or drop out. You might pick up friends for a week, a month, or maybe only see them for a day. Some you may never see again. But the ones you do see, you become fast friends. You're both in the same boat, hiking the same trail, the same miles, the same rocks, the same mountains. You build a kinship. And Hikernutt is one of those people. She's an interesting person. Despite her age, she has a way of connecting with many different people.

I really wanted to have friendships, something that lasts longer than just the trail, and there are a few I stay in contact with to this day. And that means a lot.

LAURALEE

This is so true. We've finished the Smokies together and now are at Hot Springs. I watch Hikernutt and Paul Bunyan chase each other around the outfitter's store with toy pop guns. Oh the joy found in lasting friendships, especially out here in no man's land, i.e. the Appalachian Trail. But like life, even that can change when we least expect it. After exiting the Smokies, Hikernutt develops issues with her foot, requiring her to leave the trail to have it examined. With great reluctance we part company at Hot Springs. I remain hopeful I will see her farther along the trail, that her friendly face will appear when I least expect it. But there are plans and seasons for everything under the sun, including friendships. Hikernutt was there for a particular season, to help me through the Smokies. Now I return to this lonely hike on a wilderness trail to a future filled with uncertainty, wondering what will happen next.

CHAPTER SIX

APRIL SHOWERS
SNOW SHOWERS, THAT IS

TENNESSEE

"It is safer to wander in God's woods than to travel on black highways or to stay at home."

~ John Muir, *Our National Parks*, 1901

Let's face it. Taking six months out of life to hike the Appalachian Trail is not a normal, everyday activity. There must be some element of adventure within a person to forsake all he or she knows, escape the modern world, and get down and dirty for days on end. For me, the idea of adventure started at a young age. If it wasn't some spaceship I hoped would whisk me away to some uncharted planet, it was the adventure of everyday life. I remember telling my husband when we were newly married that I didn't want to live a boring life in a home surrounded by a white picket fence. I wanted to do so much more with this short life I have. Of course that's not to say that taking care of a home and raising a child isn't an adventure all itself. It surely is. But back then I possessed a yearning for adventure outside the normal walls of a home and family. An open place yet to be filled by some act of exploration.

So here I am, hiking the Appalachian Trail with my teen son. At this stage in the hike, I've already experienced a few small "adventures." Glasses and tent poles breaking. Legs giving out. The desire to quit. But these are more like nuisances. Tests that are eventually passed. I have yet to experience anything death defying. I suppose I think life should also have some elements likened to a thriller novel or Hollywood flick. It's interesting to think about, but do I really want to experience it?

For me, as a mom hiking with her teen son, a better example of realistic, death-defying adventure is wondering if your flesh and blood is safe and sound somewhere along the trail. Rarely do my son and I actually hike together. Most days we don't see each other after we part ways in the morning and until we meet up at the shelter or camping area selected for that night. Many times I wondered and worried over Paul Bunyan's well-being. Did he take a fall somewhere and now lay injured? Or gotten off trail and lost in the woods. Whenever he's running late to a planned destination, the hiker communication network comes in handy during times of anxiety. I ask hikers that come along, "Have you seen Paul Bunyan? When did you pass him? How's he doing?"

One day when the nagging concern of a mother arises, I make the decision to wait as long as it takes for him to appear. I find a nice log to rest against where I drift off to sleep. Forty-five minutes later I awake to find there's still no sign of him. Now I'm really worried. Surely he should have caught up to me by now. Where could he be?

Finally some hikers pass by. I immediately ask the usual questions. Yes, they have seen him. One said he'd been taking off his pack numerous times, like it was bothering him. I wonder what that means. True he isn't carrying the world's fanciest pack. We bought it for him a few years back. At the time it was the newest and greatest pack on the market, but in the course of a few years, it had become rather worn. I now envision him upset over his ancient pack, maybe even wishing he could toss it over some rocky precipice.

After an hour passes, I haul on my pack and set out, determined to find him. I begin retracing my steps until I hear singing down the trail. Paul Bunyan is bellowing a tune to his MP3 player. Instead of rejoicing, I'm angry. How could he be singing, and when I have been waiting over an hour for him to show up? I expend energy reserves to find him when I need every ounce of power to hike. Come to find out, he's needed to stop and use the woods several times after suffering a stomach ailment. I immediately chastise myself for being judgmental and instead am thankful he's all right. Soon we're back hiking the trail, but motherly concern continues to well up in ways I never anticipated.

So far on this hike we've been fortunate in the weather department. The Smokies reigned in clear and unseasonably warm. There has been very little precipitation. Now I look to April and Easter weekend where I'll spend time with Steve near Erwin, Tennessee. When we arrive, homes sport brightly colored tulips and daffodils announcing spring's arrival. But the weather soon decides to do something more drastic. Like snow! Yes, snow in April and on Easter weekend of all things. We take a day to hike without our packs (called slackpacking) and trudge through a thick blanket of snow. It looks like Christmas out here rather than Easter with frosted pines reminiscent of a Currier and Ives print. Back in town, the pretty tulips and daffodils droop under the weight of frozen temperatures. But they remain vivid reminders of the promise of rebirth, the resurrection, and hope renewed, even if they are being tested by a taste of winter.

Steve soon departs, and we face a snow-filled trail. April showers are supposed to usher in May flowers. So what do snow showers bring? Soggy, cold feet for one thing, despite the fact my boots have waterproof lining. I wouldn't have minded the snow and cold so much were it not for the notorious mountain looming ahead of us. Roan Mountain, elevation 6,285 feet. From a distance I can see the mountain covered in white, with snow that can surpass calf-high in depth. And I worry.

We endure our coldest night to date with temperatures that dip well into the teens. I set up my tent on the one small patch of bare ground I find. Other hikers claim the windy shelter. The next morning we take our time packing up as we have a short day to reach the shelter just before ascending Roan Mountain. Accompanying us on this section is a hiker we met on our very first day on the trail, White Crow. He was hanging out in a trailside shelter when we hiked by on our way to Springer. Since then we keep bumping into him in unexpected places, which can happen as hikers slow down or speed up on the trail. It proves a providential twist as we are knitted with those who help us on our walk. We had Flint and Dr. B that first week out of Springer Mountain. I had Hikernutt in the Smokies.

Now for the next few days it will be White Crow. He loves to hike—or rather jog—the trail miles, carrying his backpack with a rain cover over it (which he uses even on bright, sunny days). When he senses my trepidation at ascending a snow-covered Roan Mountain, he joins me for the climb. As I hike, I gain confidence in the slushy terrain. But I take a wrong turn at the summit with the white blazes obliterated by snow covering the tree trunks. White Crow finds me then and guides me down a logging road where I intersect the trail at Carver's Gap. Hooray for a hiker angel in disguise.

After the gap is a series of windswept balds with clear skies promising stupendous views. But the snow, nearly two feet deep, fills the trench made by the many feet traversing the trail over the passage of time. Beauty, the scenery; the Beast, a snow-filled trail that soaks one's feet. Even with cold, wet feet and hiking poles in hand, I turn to gaze at the view of a snow-covered Roan Mountain in all its magnificence. While I'm standing in that thoughtful pose, an older gentleman with a camera cautiously approaches and asks if he might take my picture. He says he's from a university, and he wants to use the picture in a brochure. I'm not sure if I believe him or not but agree to the whirlwind photo shoot on a blustery day. I do wonder if my mugshot is indeed in some university website or pamphlet, and hopefully not with the caption: *Will she or won't she make it? You decide.*

Under the warmth of the sun's rays that afternoon, the snow-filled trail rapidly fills with mud and melting snow. The footing turns treacherous. There's a two mile descent before I reach the shelter area for the night. Falling on one's face is an ever-present fear in a hiker's mind. One devastating fall can take you out of this 2,000-mile marathon. It could wreck an ankle, twist a knee, or worse. Prayer for safety is on my mind as I plod along.

Despite the terrain, I manage to make good time to our next stopping place for the night at Overmountain Shelter—a red barn with two levels, converted into a hiker shelter. The first floor of the barn still contains snow from the Easter storm. The skies now rapidly fill with threatening storm clouds. Winds buffet the structure. Boards creak and groan. I'm not concerned, though. We're safe and out of the elements. I take stock of my food supply, noting that we have just enough to hold us until we can pick up our food drop the next day at noon. No problem.

The wind continues to pick up during the night. It whistles through the eaves. The whole place groans in protest. We awake the next morning to find the series of balds called the Humps completely fogged in. A high wind continues to buffet our shelter. Fellow hiker White Crow advises us not to attempt crossing the balds in this kind of weather. He's been here before, and it's not safe. But I see no choice. With our food running low, we need to head for the road crossing and the supplies waiting for us. *How hard can it be to go a mere nine miles?*

We head out into the storm and are immediately greeted by the full force of sixty-mile-per-hour winds in a cold rain and fog. We're in a battle with the elements, tossed to and fro like we're made of paper. I can barely see but a few hundred feet. The thought that we could lose the trail in the thick fog becomes a real possibility.

"Mom, we can't do this!" Paul Bunyan yells above the roar of the wind that tries to drive us to the ground. "We can't go on. We have to go back to the barn."

I begin to fuss. I want so desperately to go on. Giving up in my quest to reach that road crossing is NOT an option in my book. But there are two of us in this party, and one happens to be my sixteen-year-old son. I still need to look out for him. With a heavy heart I turn around and head back to the red barn. When I arrive, White Crow and several other guys are hanging out in the attic, watching our defeat through an open window. They don't say anything either when tears of frustration spill out of me. They quietly agree that it's the right thing to do on a day like today.

But now I face a major dilemma. Yes, we are in shelter, even if the wind and rain are coming through the airy slats of the old building. But our provisions are dangerously low. Pulling out the near empty food bags, I find one granola bar, one instant breakfast, and a packet of cheese crackers. No dinner to speak of. And I have a teenage son and myself to feed until noon tomorrow when we will pick up our food drop. Reality stares me full in the face. I don't have enough food to carry us through.

Never in my life have I ever experienced hunger. I've always had plenty of good food in a warm, comfortable atmosphere. In this drafty barn it's cold, windy, and rainy. The old wooden slats do nothing to keep the elements from coming in and soaking us. Along with the cold and dampness, our stomachs ache for want of nourishment.

The final kicker for me as a mom is when my son sits down beside me, leans his head on my shoulder and says, "Mom, I'm cold, and I'm really hungry."

His words break my heart. Tears fill my eyes when I realize I have no food to give him. Words can hardly describe the feeling of helplessness and worry that overwhelms me. We will have to divide our food between us and somehow make it last for three meals. I know too I will need to give most of my portion to my son. I sense then what the pioneers of old must have endured. The mother heading West in a wagon train on the Oregon Trail, having to divvy the meager foodstuffs among her children who stare at her with large eyes, their dirty hands clutching their aching tummies. I had a small sense of the hunger faced in third-world nations ravaged by disease, famine, and natural disasters.

Could the Appalachian Trail be teaching me things I never anticipated learning? What it means to be hungry. What it means to rely on others. Having to go to someone and ask, "Can you spare a granola bar?" Accepting the generosity of hikers like Patrick who gives us a packet of noodles out of his own supply so we have food for dinner. Or the hiker called Micro who gives us an energy bar. And then White Crow who makes us a huge pot of oatmeal and gives my son cheese crackers and a candy bar. (He remembered the plea Steve asked him way back in Georgia...to watch over us.) Hikers helping hikers in their time of need. I shiver and pace about the barn to keep warm. It feels like an eternity just waiting for dinnertime to arrive so we can cook the blessed noodles given to us by Patrick. When the time does come, Paul Bunyan and I hunker over our small stove, the steam caressing our faces, salivating over that tiny pot of bubbling noodles. It's like watching the best show on earth. The anticipation is beyond mere written words and hard to imagine even now as I write this.

JOSHUA

You always hear on the trail how food is the first thing on your mind. But there are only two main times of hunger that I recall—and one of them is Overmountain Shelter. When you realize there are only two "humps" of mountains in the way of food, but you have no way of crossing them, it's frustrating. Trying to walk up the trail and being pushed back by hurricane-force winds, you know there is no way you're gonna make it. It's one of the few times on the trail I lost hope. Sitting in that cold shelter all day, hearing the wind, feeling the rain coming up from between the floorboards, wet, tired, hungry, it is one of the most miserable moments of the hike. Even the generosity of hikers giving up some food didn't really help much.

It isn't until the next morning when I look outside to see a cloudless day and beautiful sunrise that I knew I would finish this trail. If God can get me through something this hard and bring a beautiful day to make up for it—I know He will get us through the rest of the way.

LAURALEE

The next morning we safely arrive at the road crossing and our resupply at the hostel down the road. We cook up a large batch of eggs and spam and enjoy the blessing of a warm sanctuary.

It took a day like Overmountain Shelter to realize how much we do have and to not lose sight of a thankful heart, both for food and most of all, for generous hikers. A good lesson to learn on a journey such as this.

CHAPTER SEVEN

JUST A TOUCH OF LOVE

VIRGINIA

"It's not the mountain we conquer, but ourselves."

~ Edmund Hilary, first to summit Mount Everest

When you enter a covenant with your Maker to leave home and venture to a land you know so little about, there's bound to be repercussions for your decision. Sometimes one of the results is that nagging feeling similar to Dorothy's in *The Wizard of Oz*. She tells everyone she meets along the yellow brick road, "I want to go home." At times I agree. *Someone please point me toward home. Help me get home, to that place of familiarity, where it's safe and warm, free of bugs, rain, cold, heat, hunger.*

No, I've not been transported by cyclone to some magical land with a yellow brick road now called the Appalachian Trail, though I am far away from family, home, and friends. This transportation to the wilderness is a cyclone of my own making. So far on the hike there have been great things that have happened and also the not so great. Yet in the back of my mind remains the prickly idea of home as a place of refuge. It was never that strong in the beginning of the hike, mostly because hiking was still fresh and lively. But when one trudges along on a trail day after day, doing the same thing over and over, boredom can set in. A typical day consists of hike, stop, eat, hike some more, stop, eat, sleep, then get up and do it all over again. Day in and day out, unless there's a rest break in town.

For many hikers trying to hike the whole trail at one time, Virginia becomes the state of monotony and singing the blues. Virginia is the largest state on the Appalachian Trail, all 580-plus miles of ups and downs, interspersed with crossing green valleys to reach the next ridge of mountains. It sounds new and fresh. For many hikers though, Virginia is the same territory, the same trail, the same routine day after day. It becomes the ground of decision-making. Is this hike worth it? Do I really want to go on? Virginia takes its toll as many do elect to leave, letting their dream succumb to the blues syndrome that can easily inflict an unsuspecting hiker.

Virginia to me is the state I call home. I'm not concerned about the blues, or so I think. But even before I reach the state line, we endure yet another unexpected April snowstorm that blankets the mountains in powdery white. It also turns the trail to slush when the sun's rays touch the ground. No boot can stay dry, even the waterproof ones made of the magical fabric called GORE-TEX. If there's a band of snow running along the ridgeline—flanked by thorny bushes—the snow is the Appalachian Trail. We meander through the deepest snowdrifts created by a relentless wind. The snow brings out another sneak attack of the mind. Especially the night I must dig out a spot in the snow with a broken shovel to erect our tent. The shelter that evening is packed with hikers seeking refuge. We pitch our tent on a snowy incline, using Paul Bunyan's backpack against the tent wall to prevent us from rolling down the slippery slope in our sleep. How apropos to this adventure thus far. There have been many slippery slopes by way of challenges thrust across our path. So far

God's hand has kept us from sliding into a pit of despair. If only I could remember that in the days to come.

For now, crossing the state line into Virginia is a reason to cheer, as it brings us ever closer to the ultimate goal of finishing. It makes it special too, knowing we walked from Georgia to our native state by means of muscle power alone. We enter Damascus, known as the friendliest town on the Appalachian Trail, eager for a rest break. But a strange eeriness has descended upon the town. Just two days prior, we learned of the horrific shooting at Virginia Tech that left many students and teachers dead.

On the trail, news like this can seem a world away, but in actuality it's right at our back door with the trail not far from the college. (A group from Virginia Tech helps maintain a part of the trail in the area.) We heard about the tragedy from two hikers who picked up a radio broadcast. The day we arrive in Damascus, we're met by a certain stillness as if the town were in mourning. We spend some thoughtful time in the library reading about the tragedy and sharing in the moment. Later on in our journey we will venture with friends to the memorial set up at Virginia Tech and share in a time of reflection for those who lost their lives in a senseless act. The trail may be remote, but it can draw people together in times of need.

While we are in Damascus, Steve arrives unexpectedly to whisk me away on a business trip to West Virginia. I'm transported by another cyclone, this time off the trail into the whirlwind of civilization. I admit I enjoy it immensely, with a warm hotel room, plenty of food, and no tenting in the snow. Maybe I'm enjoying it too much as the comfort ushers in thoughts of home, away from the pain, the wet feet, the cold temperatures, and the snow. The more I think about it, the more I decide I'd like to go home for a few days. I can touch base with my friends and tell them how the journey is progressing. I can bask in the luxury of a deep mattress, a warm shower, and a recliner to rest my aching feet and back. I can spend time considering, too, the tragedy of the Virginia Tech massacre and what others are going through instead of being caught up in my own little world of hiking.

I'm certain Steve will agree to my sentiment if the right words are conveyed. Except that I did do something proactive before undertaking this journey. Maybe it was the gift of intuition at work. Before the hike began, I told Steve that even if I beg to go home, *don't let me*. Why I said it at the time, I'm not sure...until it becomes clear at this moment when I tell him my idea of going home. He shakes his head and reminds me that we're supposed to do some backpacking as a family for a few days. We plan to hike the Mount Rogers National Recreation area and a picturesque part of the trail through Grayson Highlands State Park, complete with wild ponies and rugged scenery. Maybe he knows that if I do leave the trail, I might not return. And he could be right. I swallow down the disappointment and look to the family time we plan to spend out on the trail. No more ideas of home sweet home. Instead it's a continuation of an unpredictable trail.

We set out and find a spectacular place to camp one of the nights, by a raging spring with a breathtaking sunset that sets the valley aglow. Despite the beauty I see and the rest I had in Damascus, I sense weariness. Little do I realize it, but I'm showing symptoms of the Virginia blues syndrome. It's hard to describe the malady, but the symptoms are clear. Everything bothers me. The trail is the same, mostly ups, some downs, interspersed with rocks and roots. The views are the same. I've seen enough mountains to last a lifetime. The discomfort of the backpack, the aches and pains of which I used to shrug away, weighs me down. Every sensation is like a knife jabbing me. The trail appears endless in its monotony and its affliction.

Then there is the company I'm keeping. I should be thrilled to hike with my husband, the one who gave up a great deal so I can accomplish this dream of mine. But his presence only rubs me the wrong way. He is very slow. He asks me to wait for him on nearly every mountain summit. (He dislikes hiking alone.) What used to be quick mileage now takes us twice as long. My frustration mounts. Patience should be an easy virtue to acquire, but along with the other symptoms of the blues, patience is severely lacking.

After a few days we come to the place where Steve has left the van for his return home. I wait for him and Paul Bunyan as he's promised to bring a few drinks from the cooler. The heat builds on this particularly warm day. I plop down on a large rock amid the horse plops from the wild ponies to take a break in what little shade is available. I'm weary, full of questions, and growing impatient. After an hour passes, and filled with frustration, I throw on my pack and strike out after them. When we finally do meet, Steve has done a jog from the van with cold drinks tucked in his backpack, arriving like some conquering hero. But I'm in no mood to accept his generosity. The flesh is winning this battle, and it's not pretty. Angry words fly like stinging bees. Paul Bunyan is not happy with what he sees and decides to take off down the trail alone. The family is disintegrating before my eyes, and it's my fault.

When Steve leaves for home, I take stock of what's happened inside me the last few days. I realize pretty quickly that I've been foolish. I've allowed the blues to ruin the family time we were supposed to have in a picturesque area that many hikers say is one of the most scenic places on the Appalachian Trail. Of course there's mercy and grace even in weakness, but I feel guilty nonetheless. I call Steve on the cell phone to tell him my contemplation and to ask for his forgiveness. He grants it at the drop of a hat. I then strike out after Paul Bunyan and meet up with him at the next shelter where we also share words of reconciliation.

The whole scenario reminds me how much God does for

us, yet we hardly ever acknowledge it or even see it. We need a clearer vision—to see His love for us in the good things He does rather than being wrapped up in our own little cocoon of selfishness. Some say you must conquer the physical mountains to master this trail. I say you must conquer the mental mountains that are more troublesome than anything the Appalachian Trail can throw at you. Mental trials or trails are just as steep, rocky, and unpredictable, causing you to sweat and burn and feel as though you have come to the end of yourself. You're forced to let it go or risk surrendering your dreams and the ones you love. And I choose to let it go and seek family unity. All for one and one for all. It's the only way to get through the tough things in life.

Blissful's husband Steve was there with a helping hand along with his triathlon event to see his family on the trail.

For Steve's part, he continues his acts of heroism when I need it. At the Partnership Shelter, I face a new issue when I develop sudden foot pain. I run scared, especially knowing what happened to my friend Hikernutt and her foot, which ultimately forced her off the trail. Many hikers quit their hikes not just for emotional blues but for real blues like that of bruises, muscle problems, and the dreaded foot pain of plantar fasciitis. I fear I may be developing this condition. Sure, I can get scared by weather. Or eyeglasses breaking. Strange noises outside my tent. Being stranded in a cold and drafty barn without food. But it's the physical calamity that could halt this whole thing dead in its tracks.

I've already witnessed the power of prayer on this journey. For companionship, for clear weather, for food. Now I could use a miracle for my hurting foot. I call Steve on the payphone at the ranger station and find comfort in the words he offers. Like an umbrella or a waterproof jacket, prayer protects you from the deluge in a storm, keeping you safe and warm, shielding you from fear and doubt that can cripple an endeavor. I tell him about my painful foot. He says a humble prayer.

Instantly the pain is gone. I don't want to just treat this intervention of God as simply another miracle. Rather, it's a special miracle that keeps me walking on this path. A special intervention just for me. It says loudly that God cares. He heals. He loves. He helps plain ol' ordinary me do a miraculous feat by bringing special people to help me walk the trail.

Steve continues to have his own time of miraculous feats. Like the day he decides he's going to meet us after work on a Friday, in some obscure area close to the West Virginia border. He's got it all figured out. He'll drive to point A and leave the van. He'll then ride an old bicycle he bought at a yard sale (and never used once) on a ten-mile roundabout journey to Point B where the Appalachian Trail intersects the road. He will stash the bicycle in the bushes then proceed to hike five miles uphill to Point C and the shelter where Paul Bunyan and I plan to stay for the night. He calls it his personal triathlon to see his wife and son.

I call it plum crazy.

On the day he's set to perform this test of physical endurance, I call him on the cell phone to check on his progress. It's already 5 p.m., and he has not even reached Point A where he plans to leave the van. I tell him not to bother coming. It's way too late, and he'll never find the shelter in the dark. We hang up disagreeing. I don't know if he's coming or not. I still wonder about it when Paul Bunyan and I arrive at the Jenkins Shelter. At 9 p.m. and already past my bedtime, I crawl into the tent for the night. I just begin to settle in when a commotion erupts outside the camp.

"Is there a shelter here?" a familiar voice shouts.

Steve arrives like the cavalry in the dead of night, wet with perspiration, breathing heavily, carrying a daypack filled with goodies. He comes as the triumphant conqueror of the Appalachian Trail triathlon, driving, biking and hiking his way to see his loved ones. He tells us of his hair-raising time on the bicycle, careening out of control down some winding mountain road. He describes the trail up the mountain and how it had been rerouted, nearly causing him to miss the side trail to the shelter.

I have to admit, his feat stuns me. What is it when someone says they will do anything for love? To go to the extreme with an act that overcomes any obstacle and accomplishes the impossible. I'm even more amazed the next day when I see for myself what Steve endured in the bike and hike part under the cover of darkness.

Perhaps there is a cure for those Virginia blues after all. Love provides the antidote. Love in the form of athleticism— from running with drinks, to a prayer marathon, to a triathlon-type feat. Love that brings about personal and spiritual renewal when life is at its lowest. Love that outshines any darkness. Love that makes the impossible possible. Maybe that's why God says the greatest of these is love.

CHAPTER EIGHT

THE GREATEST FEAR

VIRGINIA, PART II

"One's destination is never a place but rather a new way of looking at things."

~ Henry Miller, American author

Fear, fear, the terrible thing, the more one sees, the more one dreads. Fear is a constant companion attached to my heels as I walk, like the shadow Wendy sewed onto Peter Pan's feet. Especially the fear of suffering an injury so crippling that it forces me to abandon a dream and return home in defeat. Toying with injury is a tried and true fact of a hiker's life. There are mental and physical challenges, of course. But an injury can make or break a hike. People plan a hike for months, even years, and then an injury comes along and the dream is snatched away.

Not long ago we discovered through the hiker grapevine that our first hiking buddy from the Springer Mountain, Dr. B, suffered a hairline fracture of his ankle while in the Smokies and was forced to abandon his hike. Hikernutt, the wonderful lady whose friendship I cherished in the Smokies, suffered a persistent foot injury that eventually brought her quest to a premature end. There are other hikers I learn of whose injuries forced them to quit their hikes and go home.

Up until this point, both Paul Bunyan and I have had a few incidents with potential injury. A knee problem here. Foot pain there. A few falls with ensuing strains. For me, the fear of falling outweighs the fear of an overuse injury. When slogging through a foot of snow straight downhill, the trail forces me to face falling head-on so I don't end up head-over-heels. I use skills learned on the journey to navigate the rough terrain, like hiking poles as balancing rods when rocks and roots try to disrupt the flow. I credit my hiking poles with helping me avoid numerous falls. They look like objects one attributes more to skiing than to hiking, but they assist in ascents and especially descents which can wreak havoc on tender knees. They also serve as decent brakes when the feet are going too fast for the body and a fall might be imminent.

But falls do happen, despite one's best effort. I suffered the spill back in North Carolina that wrenched a thigh muscle and left it tender for a few days. I took another spill on a twenty-mile trek just a week ago on rocks still slick after a heavy rainfall. I got up, none the worse for the wear, except that falling with a thirty-plus-pound pack strapped to my back makes it tough to clamber easily to my feet. Like life, when you fall down, you pick yourself up—baggage and all—and learn from it. Like how to avoid a rock or root that tries to trip you up. Or by taking it slower, planting your feet correctly, and using your poles as makeshift anchors. To not get ahead of the game but to be careful and conscientious.

JOSHUA

Honestly, I was pretty blessed not to be seriously injured on the trail. Now of course, hiking along a hazardous trail, accidents can and will happen. Other than the occasional thorn scratch and rock in the shoe, I only suffer a few "major" injuries. Walking quickly while carrying a heavy backpack, you're guaranteed to lose your balance and fall at least once or twice. Of course the trail is nice enough to put some sharp rocks right where my knee landed on a particular fall. I have to say the sensation of pulling a rock out of your flesh is not a fun experience. Neither is seeing blood trickling down your leg. Knowing you still have to hike twelve miles and your knee is bleeding more and more...those days are not the best. But those are the times you just have to buck up, stick a bandage on it, and move on.

LAURALEE

I try not to think about what might happen to this whole game plan if one of us suffers a serious injury that takes us off the trail. I don't like delving into speculation. It can rob you of peace and leave you anxious about tomorrow. We're not supposed to worry about tomorrow but to let tomorrow take care of itself. That goes for falls and injuries.

So what happens the next day? I strain my Achilles tendon on rocks near a formation called the Dragon's Tooth. The cause? Hiking too fast on uneven terrain. My foot gets caught between the rocks, and I wrench my calf. It hurt like the dickens for a time, but slowly the pain goes away. I feel a momentary sigh of relief that the injury won't threaten the hike. I push any sickening sensation of fear to the dark recesses of my mind where it belongs.

Now I look ahead to the next section of trail that wanders into the Blue Ridge Mountains and ascends to the Blue Ridge Parkway. A new destination comes to mind—Crabtree Falls Road—where Steve will pick us up for a week of respite at home. I need to do some editing on books for my publisher and take time to meet with friends and update everyone on our progress. I can't wait. I plan to herald from the very housetop, *Look at me, everyone! Look how far I've come!*

Here I am, all the way from Georgia. I've made it...well, I'm getting there....slow but sure.

One of the most famous places to have one's picture taken on the AT atop McAfee Knob in Virginia

My eagerness to get there propels me to take the trail a bit too fast for comfort. And then it happens.

Jerk. Spasm. Pain.

I halt. My right calf is in spasms, sending pain running down the length of my outer tibia. I try to stretch out the offending muscle. *Okay, I get the message. Enough racing the hills. Time to put a lid on my eagerness. Calm it down.* I soak the affected extremity in every cold stream I come to. I try bargaining with the injured leg. *Please, don't do this to me now! We're nearly home, and then I can rest.* But the pain persists. I don't like it; especially when I recall what happened at Dragon's Tooth for those few painful seconds. Fear grips me. If this is an Achilles tendon injury, my hike is finished. What an awful feeling this is. It's worse than the pain of the injury.

I take it easy the rest of the day and make it to the shelter for the night. I hope this calf thing is like any other nuisance I've had to deal with. I will contact Steve, he'll pray, and presto, it will all go away. I manage to get ahold of him on the cell phone and tell him what's happened. He does the usual prayer thing, but there is no change. Well, there's always tomorrow, I suppose.

The next day I plan to give myself plenty of time to hike, along with taking numerous rest stops. For the first few hours everything seems fine. The worst must be over. And then it hits again, that painful spasm in the calf. It's a wrenching of muscle against tendon, tendon against bone. Clearly something is wrong.

I'm devastated. I sit down at a trail intersection to wait for Paul Bunyan who is carrying the cell phone. I hope I can reach Steve to come bail us out. We'll only be stopping our hike a few days earlier than expected, I reason. I try to stay positive but fear tugs at my heels. Is this the end...like so many other hikers who had to get off in Virginia because of the blues or problems or injuries? Will I be another casualty to the trail in my home state?

Paul Bunyan arrives, and he too is complaining of some leg pain. While we wait for our ride, Paul Bunyan cooks up some soup for lunch.

I feel like it's my farewell meal to an unaccomplished dream. I don't want this to happen. But I've come too far not to realize that this whole adventure of mine is really in God's hands. I make the plans; He must direct the steps. And right now, for some reason, my steps have been halted. I will have the muscle checked out at a sports clinic. I will do what I need to do to heal quickly and return to the trail. That's the way it's gonna be.

I hope and pray.

Paul Bunyan cooks lunch on our little stove

* * * * *

After being home a few days, there's good news to report. The sports doctor determines I suffered a minor tear in the calf muscle and to stay off it a week before slowly resuming my hike. I like that kind of diagnosis. At least I'll be able to continue the journey north, when the calf muscle is ready.

In the meantime, Paul Bunyan and I share about our hike with others. Before our hike, I arranged with my neighbor to stay in touch with her son's second-grade class concerning our adventure. I've sent postcards to the class whenever we cross a state line, along with fun facts about trail life, wildlife, etc. Now the kids are eager to see us up close and personal—to put faces behind those postcards and hear tales of an adventure in the making.

With a desire to make this a fun time, we gather our gear along with pictures from our hike. Students and teachers alike stare as we march into the school, backpacks on, carrying hiking poles. In the classroom, the excitement is palpable. The little kids laugh when Paul Bunyan snuggles into his sleeping bag and zips it all the way up mummy-style.

We show them our little stove and cooking supplies. We tell them what we ate. We then show pictures of the state lines we crossed, the snowy trails, the places we've seen. The kids love it. A week later they send us a cute handmade book of illustrated papers they had written about their trail names. It's a book I treasure to this day.

Once my leg heals, Paul Bunyan and I give consideration to the next section of trail in Virginia—a hundred-mile stretch needed to complete this monstrously large state. We make plans at various times to hike it, only to face one medical setback after another. Paul Bunyan gets the stomach flu. I come down with a nasty cold. I'm left wondering if our hike will ever continue.

We finally decide the best way to complete this section of the trail is to hike it in chunks rather than in one long trip. We will connect one portion at a time until we form a perfect chain of completion. I begin by testing my injured leg on a short, four-mile section. We hike another ten miles with friends from church who are eager to experience a part of the famous trail that we've been traversing these many months. We also take a break from hiking to attend the festival of the year—Trail Days—held each May in Damascus, Virginia. Many hikers come off the trail to attend and march in the hiker parade. It's an opportunity to reunite with friends formed by the tough battle of hiking the Appalachian Trail.

I head to the festival anticipating a reunion, and I'm not disappointed. I see Flint from our first week on the trail. I run into my old buddy, Hikernutt, from the Great Smoky Mountain days. I even see White Crow from those snowy days in the Roan Mountain area. Those hikers made a huge difference in this venture. But as I talk with others and share in the excitement, I wonder if I will really finish this trail. It still appears a lofty goal at best, especially as a head cold now begins to settle on me.

As we stumble into an area of the festival called tent

city where hikers stay during the three-day event, we come across a hiker wearing a huge green hat encircled with green ribbon. I recognize him as a past hiker we met on our very first night at the Springer Mountain Shelter. He'd been there celebrating with other hikers from the previous year's class. His trail name is appropriate for his attire. Leprechaun. But it's the words he says that really intrigue me, even if he is a bit tipsy from drinking beer.

"I have to tell you something." He looks at me intently. "We were going through the trail journals for the hikers this year. (I have been keeping an online trail journal of my hike so far, including pictures taken along the way.) We were trying to decide from the list of hikers who will make it all the way this year."

I'm listening, wondering what he's going to say.

"We made it like a game," Leprechaun continues. "And guess what? I chose you to make it out of them all. And you know why?"

I couldn't begin to imagine why.

"Because you had a picture of me in your online trail journal, standing in front of the Springer Mountain Shelter." He grins in impish fashion. "That's why!"

I suppose a tipsy leprechaun thinks he is our lucky charm. (He even reminds me a little of the goofy guy on the Lucky Charms cereal box.) But his words stick with me. *I chose you to make it out of them all.* I ponder that during the rest of the event, even as my head cold comes on full force. Stifling a sneeze and nursing an awful sore throat, I try to agree. But sometimes this dream still seems farfetched. Even though I've completed close to half the trail, Maine might as well be a planet in a far-off galaxy. Can I really believe the words of some tipsy leprechaun in his green hat?

A week later, after chipping away at the trail in Virginia, we cross the bridge over the James River, the final section we need to complete the state. (We already hiked the

Shenandoahs and northern Virginia to get ready for this adventure.)

Six states are done. Eight more to go.

But an unpredictable sign lies before me.

Caution! Untold danger lies ahead on the journey of life. Man your prayer stations and read your instruction manual on how to conquer the navigational hazards ahead. And may the God of the Universe be with you.

CHAPTER NINE

ROCKS AND TICKS AND RATTLERS
OH, YEAH...

PENNSYLVANIA

"One step at a time is good walking."

~ Chinese Proverb

The first two quarters have been played. It's halftime, and the game is tied. We are settling in to play the third and fourth quarters in this GaMe called hiking the Appalachian Trail. There have been a few touchdowns. A few penalties by way of weather and mental attitudes. Times of injury. But now we are driving toward the goal of winning—climbing Katahdin in Maine and standing at the trail's northern terminus. But that is still over a thousand miles away. At this point I feel if I can make it through Pennsylvania, I can make it the rest of the way. Or at least give the impression I can make it.

Pennsylvania to the Appalachian Trail hiker holds a bit of a nasty reputation in the form of rocks. Now if you ask the residents if they think they're being treated unfairly on account of the rock situation, you might hear differently. But I've seen photos of the terrain taken by other hikers. I know those beastly rocks are out there.

I wonder how well my new gear will work now that I'm using a brand-new pack and wearing new trail shoes. Because of my calf injury, I elect to try trail runners. To the untrained eye, the sheer notion of a hiker clad in running shoes doesn't bode well for avoiding injury. It only appears to serve new issues, especially in the rocky terrain that looms ahead. But others swear by them. The running shop where I purchased them even claimed that my boots probably contributed to my calf situation. They say these shoes are more stable. I decide to give them a try and see what happens.

I also trade in my heavy-duty backpack for a more compact, lighter model. Since we're entering the summer months of hiking where one switches to a forty-degree sleeping bag and summer clothing, it makes sense to downsize. Steve ventured to our favorite outfitter at Rockfish Gap in Virginia to find a pack he believed would suit me perfectly. I'm dubious when he shows it to me, but he exudes confidence. He insists I try his solution for a few weeks. If I don't like the pack, he will bring back my old clunker when next we meet. "So humor me until then," he says.

I do, and it turns out to be a wise decision. I end up carrying the new pack the rest of the journey and enjoying three fewer pounds on my back.

On Memorial Day, Paul Bunyan and I cross the bridge spanning the Potomac River in Harper's Ferry, northward bound. Harper's Ferry is a quaint Civil War town that is also home to the Appalachian Trail Conservancy (ATC), the main headquarters overseeing the trail alongside the National Park Service as well as its many volunteer organizations. (Did I mention the Appalachian Trail is actually one huge national park? It's called the Appalachian National Scenic Trail.) We stop at the center for a hiking tradition—having our picture taken in front of the headquarters' sign. Now with crossing the bridge, we also cross into another state. Maryland will take us about two days to hike, then comes

Pennsylvania and the all-important halfway mark near Pine Grove Furnace State Park. It's all coming in such rapid succession, it gives the illusion we're making steady progress toward our ultimate goal. And that's good for a mental lift.

I'm not long on the trail before I realize what the summer season brings to trail life. Where there were once bare trees, leafy foliage meets my gaze. Where there was nothing but a few hairy vines snaking up certain trees, the glistening three-leaf pest of poison ivy borders the trail. Where they had once been hiding in nests and hives, insects now make an annoying appearance. Mosquitoes, deerflies, and the notorious deer ticks carrying dreaded Lyme disease are out in full force. Rattlesnakes sun atop rock piles and even on the trail itself. Nature is alive and well, enjoying the warmth of the season. It's a whole new atmosphere of hiking akin to a jungle, especially along the Potomac River when I'm immediately attacked by hungry deerflies. Six huge, red welts soon decorate the backs of my legs. So much for the natural insect repellent I'd applied that day. New tactics are required to further safeguard a soul on a wilderness journey. Out comes the full-strength DEET, my protection of choice on exposed skin.

During the week, we also encounter another first—hot, humid weather with heat indices topping one hundred degrees. At Pen Mar Park, a friendly maintenance man offers to open up the concession stand so we can purchase cold sodas. He announces to us that a heat advisory has been posted for the area. Summer is upon us, full steam ahead.

Paul Bunyan is not thrilled by the announcement. In fact, he's been downright moody lately. Suddenly he springs a new decision on me.

"Mom, I'm tired of this hiking thing. When Dad comes to see us in a few days, I'm going home."

What?

Paul Bunyan's announcement takes me completely

by surprise. Not in these many months, with the difficult weather and conditions he's faced, has he ever said anything about quitting. This is the first time his lips even mention the words.

A new panic sets in. What if he quits? What about the gear we're currently splitting between us? With my new, compact backpack, how can I handle the gear by myself, along with the extra weight?

I don't say much to his announcement. Instead I look for ways to cool off and rid our minds of the trail's toughness. Like a pizza restaurant down the road where the owner prepares a huge meat lovers pizza, with cold milkshakes for dessert. We find a nice, shady spot near Caledonia State Park to rest. We also encounter our first rattlesnake of the hike, eating its dinner of some black furry thing we can't begin to identify. I try taking a photo of it. The serpent regurgitates its dinner in an angry rattle and lifts its head to strike. We hightail it down the trail.

A few nights later I ask Paul Bunyan if he still plans to leave the trail. He shrugs and issues a quiet, "Maybe. I don't know."

Sigh.

JOSHUA

Yeah, famous last words. Looking back at it, I always wonder what I was thinking in Pennsylvania. I remember the heat, the humidity, the mosquitoes, the overgrown trails, and I remember, yeah, I'm in my right mind and thinking clearly. Who would want to be out here in this? These are the days you don't want to hike. When the trail becomes the Amazon jungle, it's just not fun anymore. But parents know exactly how to change an attitude, including a pizza stop, a milkshake, an ice-cream challenge, and a trip to Gettysburg.

But honestly, it's not all that which gets me back on the

trail. When you've spent so much time doing one specific thing, you do get homesick. But the trail is the closest thing you have to home. Being in town is nice, but being on the trail, getting the miles done and laying back in the shelter at night is a feeling that's hard to copy. And I know if I stopped now, I would regret it the rest of my life. So I plod along, knowing this is what I'm supposed to do.

LAURALEE

Without a great deal of fanfare we arrive at the noted halfway point of our journey, Pine Grove Furnace State Park. (Or just shy of the halfway point. It varies depending on the trail's length, which also varies year to year.) At the convenience store, hikers settle down at one of the outside tables to indulge in a thru hiker's tradition—consuming a half gallon of ice cream to mark the halfway point of the journey. If one succeeds in eating the half gallon of ice cream all by themselves, they are inducted into the Half Gallon Club, marked by their signature in a notebook. There's no way I can begin to eat a half gallon, so Paul Bunyan and I split one instead. But what is supposed to be a yummy, cold treat becomes a chore, trying to consume a full-fat food item on a stomach that has rarely had fat on the trail. And I don't like it, either, that I see a sign prominently posted on the bulletin board of the store, listing emergency numbers should one keel over from the challenge of overeating. I push the negativity aside. We've both finished the challenge as far as I'm concerned, both in hiking to the halfway point and eating the whole half gallon of ice cream. And we have survived.

Now I look forward to some time off with Steve. He arrives to take us to Gettysburg for a day. It's a nice change of pace after being on the trail. I enjoy the feel of town clothes and being a tourist rather than a hiker. Though it's a hot day,

I relax in our air-conditioned van as we travel from site to site. A scrumptious dinner of prime rib and lemon meringue pie tops off the day. Steve then drives us back to Pine Grove Furnace and the hostel. He prepares to leave for home, but he won't be taking Paul Bunyan with him. Young Paul's decided to hike on, and I'm mighty proud of him and relieved as well.

Two days later we're hiking through the hedgerow country of the Cumberland Valley, marked by flatlands, farm fields, and crossings over major highways. Suddenly I find myself in the first chapter of this book—a reluctant patient in the emergency room at Carlisle Medical Center. The night before, I suffered chest pain in our motel room. I awoke with it the following morning. I couldn't stand, move, or anything. Something had to be done. I managed to find an older gentleman in the motel parking lot willing to drive Paul Bunyan and me to the hospital. There they intend to rule out a heart attack. Me, a hiker of over 1,000 miles, in for heart pain.

"Are you kidding?" I say to the doctor when he tells me I need to be admitted. "It's that serious?"

"We won't know until we run some more tests. You don't want to go back out hiking with no medical help around and then drop dead. It's better to find out. Heart conditions are more difficult to diagnose in women. We don't take any chances with chest pain."

No, I certainly don't want to die hiking. I want to make it to the end and make it out alive, thank you. But lying in that bed, hooked to an IV and some heavy monitor on my chest where they can keep a watchful eye on my heart, I wonder more and more about this trail and all the situations I've faced. Thank goodness we don't know what tomorrow holds. If someone were to tell me I would be in the hospital halfway through this hike, I don't think I would have picked up my backpack or put on my shoes. If someone were to say I would be held up in a leaky barn for two days in a driving rain with no food, or have to erect a tent on a snow-covered hillside, or endure an injury to my calf, I would have told them, *nope, not me.*

Now I undergo this newest challenge, hooked up to wires, waiting for the tests to be conducted. Steve arrives from Virginia to be with me and to help get our stuff out of the motel room where we left it. I use the time to chat with a few nurses about my experience and my life as a writer. Maybe I'm going through the prep stages for some future event. Maybe I'm being prepared for a time when I can share about this journey through speaking and the written word. (And here I am!)

I endure a night of being pricked and prodded by medical personnel, followed by a nuclear stress test in the morning (of which the cardiologist appears incredulous that a fit hiker like me needs this kind of invasive screening). After the test is complete, the all-clear signal is given. I breathe a sigh of relief. Time to pack up and head for...

Where else but the Appalachian Trail? I may be one of the few thru hikers ever released from a hospital with EKG pads still stuck to various places and sporting a bandage over an IV site, hiking six miles to the next shelter. I've slowed my progress, but I refuse to stop. It's one foot in front of the other. Mile upon mile, northward bound, or as a fellow hiker Beach Bum writes in every trail register, "Staying here tonight, walking north tomorrow." And that's really what this boils down to, with some minor stories thrown in to make life interesting. We walk, we stay, we walk some more. We do the same thing day after day, week after week, month after month. Except for the rare hospital visit or some other such nuisance.

* * * * *

We pass through a few boulder fields in Pennsylvania

but nothing too spectacular to warrant the Rocksylvannia nickname given to the state. There are more encounters with rattlesnakes. Several hikers leave notes on the trail, held down by stones, warning of a particularly infested rattlesnake den north of the Peters Mountain Shelter. At first I wonder if it could be true, and if I should heed the warning. Sure enough, right in the middle of the trail, a rattler lies on an exposed rocky slab, sunning itself. I take great care to scramble down the rocky hillside, picking my way through the barricade of rocky debris just so the snake can continue its sunbathing undisturbed. So much for the idea of man ruling the beasts of the field and the crawling creatures of the earth. I must bow to the rattler's ways. For what it's worth, the snake did not even shake, rattle, or roll. In fact it probably yawned and continued enjoying the sunshine.

Besides its natural aspects, Pennsylvania is also turning out to be a state of human interest. Along with fellow hikers and the medical staff of the hospital, I meet other memorable Pennsylvanians early on who make us feel welcome. Like the worker at Pen Mar Park who opened up the concession booth to supply cold sodas to two overheated hikers. A woman out walking her dog gave us candy on a whim.

Now an unexpected surprise awaits us at a place called Swatara Gap. We cross the metal bridge to find a former thru hiker has arranged a bountiful feast of goodies spread out on a large table. It's Cadillac goods to hungry and weary hikers, with huge bottles of soda, king-sized Snicker bars (mainstay with hikers), resupply needs such as noodle packets and Pop Tarts, even fresh bananas. When I ask why he's doing this, he remarks how hikers helped him on his long hike last year. He wanted to repay the favor. And he does, with a wonderful snack break that keeps us going, and going like an installation of fresh batteries.

We welcome the pleasant break as the next section of trail is completely overgrown by thick patches of poison ivy. I'm highly allergic to the stuff yet I can't help either stepping on or brushing up against it. Oh, the challenges of trail life. To think that all we might suffer at home is a paper cut or a prick from a thorny rosebush. Out here the dangers are multiplied. They come at you in so many different ways, you're never without a challenge that tests your will and your faith.

We take a break at the next shelter from the overabundance of poison ivy and look for deer ticks no bigger than the period at the end of this sentence. There I read the shelter register and catch up on the hikers who have come before us. To my surprise, I find a message from a hiker we met on an online trail community who is looking forward to meeting us. It's nice to have a cheering squad supporting one's endeavor. I think of the marathon runners, enduring their twenty-six-mile jaunts over hill and dale, to the cheering masses greeting them at mileage markers along the way. From Georgia to Virginia, our cheering squad has been mainly my husband. But now that we're farther north, he's not as visible as he once was. In fact, the cheering section is downright quiet.

Enter the hiker called Emerald. He hiked the trail over twenty years ago when it was neither fashionable nor popular. We were introduced on the trail forum called White Blaze, and since then he's kept track of our progress. When we arrive at the 501 Shelter (5-0-1 is its name), he's there to greet us—a living, breathing cheering section along this multi-month marathon. We chat around a crackling fire. He hopes to run into us again farther down the trail. I like these breaks from hiking where one can be reenergized physically, emotionally, and spiritually. Physical = food. Spiritual = God's spirit, that heavenly wonderful Counselor. Emotional = cheering squads like Steve, Dr. B and Flint, Hikernutt and now Emerald, along with the many trail angels and townsfolk we meet along the way.

Speaking of towns, we didn't plan to stop at Palmerton, Pennsylvania, but after a few rough days on the trail with rocks and bugs, snakes and poison ivy, we yearn for a place to rest and recoup. We hike into the town of Palmerton, quite unaware of what to expect. The first greeting I receive is a cup of ice-cold lemonade from a woman at the neighborhood bank. The town continues to roll out the red carpet of hospitality with a free apple at the grocery store, a free place to stay in the basement of a building that once housed prisoners (appropriately called the Jailhouse Hostel) along with giving us a welcome bag of goodies like a new toothbrush and some bandages. A fellow hiker even treats us to a huge watermelon. What a great respite in a friendly town.

The rest stop arms us well for what northern Pennsylvania is famous for—various sizes and shapes of rocks littering the trail. Papa rocks, mama rocks, baby bear rocks. There are rocks from ankle turners to huge ledges, testing skill and the ability to leap and climb and dodge and negotiate. One must be as surefooted as those white-haired mountain goats that can cling to steep rocky areas of the Rocky Mountains. Or one can also cling to an appropriate Scripture for this terrain:

He makes my feet like hinds' feet, and will make me walk [not to stand still in terror, but to walk] and make [spiritual] progress upon my high places [of trouble, suffering, or responsibility]! (Habakkuk 3:19b).

How true. I am able to walk and make progress, and not just physical progress alone but spiritual as well. Up and over that rocky terrain of life that tries to bring defeat through sadness, doubt, fear, pain. The Appalachian Trail serves as a visual reminder of what we need to do when the going gets rough. It teaches me more than just walking from Point A to Point B. The trail is becoming a spiritual walk to understanding a bit more about God and His heart for me. And how one can be successful in accomplishing a dream.

Now as I close in on Delaware Water Gap, another victory is about to be realized. To most hikers, the gap simply marks the state line with New Jersey. Delaware Water Gap symbolizes to me a place where dreams were once kindled. I often journeyed here as a young girl with my family on our way to Shenandoah National Park. We'd stop in the camper, and I'd think about the Appalachian Trail meandering somewhere nearby. I never saw the trail, of course, but I knew it was not far away from the books I'd read. I used to wonder if and when I'd ever hike it.

Now as I hike off the ridgeline and into the town of Delaware Water Gap, I sense another milestone. Not just in finishing the rocks of Pennsylvania but the satisfaction of embracing a sought-after dream. How often does one get to experience a dream come true except in a fairy tale? If I can continue avoiding pitfalls and seek a happily-ever-after ending somewhere on a lone mountain in Maine, I might just have a winning story to cherish.

I'll have to wait and see.

CHAPTER TEN

THE UPSIDE AND THE DOWNSIDE

NEW JERSEY & NEW YORK

"Let us run with patient endurance and steady and active persistence the appointed course of the race that is set before us."

~ Hebrews 12:1b

Another state, another moment in time. One week remains before Steve rejoins us trailside to become an official northbound hiker. While he has been our supply train, taxi cab, triathlon athlete, general all-around support team and cheering squad all rolled into one, soon he will become one with us in the trail trenches. One who will experience the hardships and the good things about trail life. Steve plans to take six weeks of vacation time to hike with us through the remainder of New York and on into Connecticut, Massachusetts and Vermont. We'd planned this out ahead of time so he could be part of the experience.

But dreams are experienced in different ways by different people. Two different people. Two different goals. Two different ways to hike. I've already seen how a family member can present a trial of a different sort. It happened down in Virginia. Steve is not in the kind of condition we are, trail-hardened by the day-in, day-out toil of hiking for many months. We will need to cut back on our mileage. But I think of this as prep work, so to speak, before we tackle the most arduous part of the trail through the White Mountains of New Hampshire. To avoid a repeat of Virginia, I will ready myself mentally and emotionally by adjusting my attitude if we are to have an enjoyable experience as a family. I will put my goals on hold and let someone else's way of doing things be a part of the experience. This must be a group effort and not an individual pursuit.

Easier said than done sometimes.

I do a lot of thinking as Paul Bunyan and I cross the Delaware River into New Jersey, like George Washington did as a precursor to a vital victory in the Revolutionary War. But instead of a battle for the freedom of a nation, we hike for the freedom of the spirit that we can one day share with others.

When I think of New Jersey, immediately I think of stark gray buildings, lots of people, and limited scenery. Instead the state gives us a pleasant surprise in the form of a glacial pond to sit beside and reflect. There are lofty ridges offering views of the Delaware Valley, a high stone monument at High Point State Park that one can see for miles, and fairly tame terrain compared to other sections.

Soon we fall in with a group of new hikers called sectioners. Sectioners do a portion of the Appalachian Trail in a given time period. It can be over the course of a weekend to a week or longer. With the summer months here, section hikers use their vacation time to join in on a trail adventure. Hikers like us, trying to conquer the whole trail in one long hike, appear to be diminishing as we head north. We've not seen any northbounders since southern Pennsylvania. But we enjoy the section hikers we do meet, even as they come and go when their hikes are completed.

For a brief time the trail sneaks out of New Jersey and

into New York before crossing back over again. One morning Paul Bunyan and I head to a small town that lies within New York State called Unionville to pick up a mail drop at the post office. Mail drops are fun because empty food bags are restocked with goodies that we enjoy in abundance for the first few days. While we sort out food in front of the post office, an elderly gentleman walks up and warmly greets us. He inquires where we stayed the previous night while informing us he's the mayor of Unionville. I must say I am impressed that the man would stop to say hello to two rather odiferous wanderers. He then asks how far we plan to go.

"We're doing the whole trail," I tell him.

He shakes his head. "I know the name of a good psychiatrist in town if you want to get checked out." He grins. I smile back. A friendly mayor with a wit to boot and another memorable encounter with people we meet along the way. Even if he is singling out the madness part of our adventure!

Reunited once more with our small band of merry section hikers, we return to the New Jersey side of things, anxious to spend the night in the town of Vernon, three miles distant. Paul Bunyan and I have rarely needed to hitch for car rides on this hike. But with Vernon a good distance away, and already hiking some fourteen miles, the necessity of a hitch is looking apparent. The other section hikers are at a farmers market down the road, buying a few goodies and mingling with the customers. My mind is focused on getting to town. I tell Paul Bunyan we ought to start hitching for a ride before it gets too late. We begin heading toward the road when we're abruptly called back to the farmers market. To our delight, one of the hikers has found us all rides to Vernon.

Why do I tell this story?

We didn't realize at the time, but it's illegal to hitchhike in New Jersey. We could have been fined a couple hundred dollars for doing it.

What's the lesson learned?

Even in our ignorance, God was watching out for us. Hikers helped us when we didn't even know we needed help! What is it about the Good Shepherd who guides His sheep? Who keeps them in the right pasture and away from the bad...like inadvertently breaking a state law?

Once in Vernon (remember, I still didn't know hitchhiking is illegal), I try to figure out how to get back to the trail the next morning. Suddenly an injured hiker arrives at the hostel, one we had met a week before in Palmerton, Pennsylvania of all places. And since he can't hike, he offers us a ride in the morning. Once more our needs are met in a miraculous way. As we continue to head northward, we will become even more intimately acquainted with the Shepherd's heart for His ignorant sheep.

Glad Someone else is in control of this venture.

* * * *

We leave New Jersey for good and cross into a new state—New York, the place of my birth and also the birth of my childhood fascination with the Appalachian Trail. Straddling two state lines with one foot in New Jersey and the other in New York, I smile for the camera, happy for the progress we are making. Tomorrow I will link up with Steve and then take a three-day rest at my parents' home before hiking through New York and on into New England. I feel like much has been accomplished thus far, and I'm optimistic about the future. I believe a good deal of the bad concerning the trip has been dealt with. Bad weather. Bad health issues. Maybe even the bad bugs, though I know there are places in New England where mosquitoes greet hikers by the swarms. I still have the White Mountains looming before me, but I'm feeling fairly confident about trail life and trail walking. It's all going well.

Arriving at the first shelter in New York, we set up shop for the night. I'm in the midst of cooking dinner when I see a dog arriving ahead of his master. *Great. Some hiker has decided to drag his pooch along. It's gonna monopolize the shelter. Probably bark and become a nuisance. No sleep tonight.*

I peer a little closer to see the dog is a beagle, and it sure looks a lot like my dog, Lady. Then I hear a familiar shout from the trail. Steve arrives, a grin parked on his face. He's come a day early as a surprise and brought Lady with him until tomorrow when she will find a temporary home with my parents. Thankfully Lady adapts well to the outdoors, settling beneath the shelter for the night. We are a family once again.

The next day we climb Mombasha High Point for our first glimpse at the skyscrapers of New York City framing the horizon. It seems surreal to think I've walked some 1500 miles just to see the great city of New York. I've come so close, yet it feels so far. Lady doesn't care. She's enjoying eating homemade jerky and the thrill of a wander in the woods. It's a dog's world.

We take time away from the trail to spend with my parents before being dropped off midway through New York. Here Steve plans to hike with us for a few weeks. We squeeze our way through a barrier of rock called the Lemon Squeezer on a humid day. How do they come up with these interesting names to describe certain areas of the trail? It conjures thoughts of ice-cold lemonade.

Soon we realize the reason behind the increased humidity when the sound of distant thunder greets us. We're not far from a public swimming area called Tiorati Circle and make a mad dash for the safety of the public bathhouse before the skies open up. As I stand there under the cover of the concession building, watching the rain come down, I'm glad for safety and hope this isn't a precursor of future events filled with violent storms and heavy rain. When the clouds clear, I welcome the pleasing aroma of the woods, the way the leaves glisten with water droplets, the springs bubbling up with liquid wonder ready to replenish a thirsty soul. The storms of life can bring a fury of wind-driven rain and dangerous lightning. But they also bring refreshing, healing, rebirth, and growth. All things work together for good.

Our next destination is a popular summertime spot for city residents called Bear Mountain State Park. Here the trail winds through a busy picnic area and a wildlife exhibit filled with curious tourists and exotic animals. At various times on this hike, Paul Bunyan and I have garnered attention with our packs as we mosey through towns. But today it's Steve's turn. To help combat the age-old problem of chafing, Steve has opted to wear a hiking kilt. Such attire attracts all manner of curiosity among the young who tug on their parent's sleeve and ask, "Mommy, why is that man wearing a skirt?"

I decide the best thing to do is hike quickly through the area, past the wildlife exhibits to reach the Bear Mountain Bridge that spans the wide Hudson River. I read in journals of many a hiker who'd crossed this bridge on the Appalachian Trail. Back then they had to pay a modest toll to walk cross. We cross for free, and I savor every step that draws me closer to my destination.

So far, so good. This family adventure is going well. We've had a few days where I pull ahead of Steve while he takes his time acclimating to the PUDs of the Appalachian Trail. He is always there at the end of the hiking day and in good spirits. Until one afternoon when I arrive at Fahnestock State Park and he fails to show up. Normally I would panic. Instead I sit down to reason out his absence. I know that swimming and Steve go together. If he can find a place to take a dip, he will. I recall the state park has a huge lake. I put two and two together. When Steve finally arrives, dripping wet, my suspicions are confirmed. A dip on a hot summer's day tops his list of to-dos on the trail. My to-do list is miles. I hope our different ways of doing things will work out and not become one big tadoo.

New York also offers other pleasures for my he-man hiker in the form of culinary delights. Steve's not used to the meager rations we've been consuming since the hike began. For him, a half cup of noodles for dinner just doesn't cut it. On the Appalachian Trail, food becomes a passion. We carry what we can in our backpacks and then gorge ourselves at restaurants and delis along the way. The Appalachian Trail diet consists of eating all the junk you want in town and watching it melt away as you hike the miles. I eat things on the trail I never would eat at home. Donuts, milkshakes, cheeseburgers, double-stuffed Oreos, sugar-loaded colas. Yet the calories consumed do not begin to compare to the amount of calories being burned on a full day of hiking. It is said a hiker can burn upward of 6,000 calories a day. Trying to carry the equivalent of that many calories is impossible, so one must recoup it at stops along the way.

At the state park, Steve decides on breakfast at the concession stand. Here we feast on egg and cheese sandwiches made by the park employees. (We were the only ones around, and they were happy to oblige.) At the next road crossing, I leave Steve a note on a rock pile. Paul Bunyan and I walk down the road to get some lunch supplies at a deli, and Steve is treated to a big sandwich accompanied by potato chips. It makes for a happy husband. The final day in New York provides the bonanza in the eating department. At a road crossing, we find a hotdog stand set up at a parking pullout. The gal manning the stand has done it for several years now, and ravenous hikers are her best customers. Steve and I indulge while Paul Bunyan ventures to yet another deli to buy our second breakfast. Two meals in a row.

Then a few short miles before the Connecticut border, trail angels have set up a nice spread in the nearby woods. There are chairs, sodas, boxes of resupply items, cream cheese on bagels and fruit inside a cooler, cookies and ice-cold water.

It's either feast or famine out here, and for us, today's the feast.

What a great way to cross into our next state and be officially welcomed into New England. Katahdin, the northern terminus of the trail, doesn't seem so farfetched now. I know we still have the difficult sections to go, but for the first time I feel as if I may actually finish this trail. I know better than to raise my hopes too high. There's still a great deal left to do. Summits of great mountains with views galore to foggy and rainy descents on slippery, rocky slopes. The energy to hike two, twenty-mile days to the agony of doing just eight. Sickness, injury, rocks upon rocks, and the toughest single mile of the entire trail.

It all awaits us in New England.

CHAPTER ELEVEN

NO RAIN, NO MAINE

CONNECTICUT

"No pain, no rain, no Maine."

~ often quoted by thru hikers

I must say I've been "blissfully" blessed by weather up until this point. We've had a few run-ins with rainstorms, some snow in April, a thunderstorm or two in Pennsylvania—which we were able to outrun to the safety of trailside shelters. It's actually been a dry season, which can be good and bad. There's a saying in trail circles of *no pain, no rain, no Maine*. Rain is a necessity, but it can also be a trial. On the one hand, who likes hiking in rain? On the other hand, hikers need rain to reenergize the springs where we obtain our water. The water situation in some places has been poor with few if any springs running, particularly in New York. Trail angels have taken to leaving water containers at road crossings for thirsty hikers. The rain is definitely needed.

But rain is also tough to hike in, especially when trying to figure out what to wear. Either you get drenched by the rain or drenched by sweating in some supposedly breathable rain jacket. The jacket retains the stale, moist air you exude from the exercise of climbing the mountain peaks. A hiker then ends up more drenched on the inside than on the outside. Since it's summer and hypothermia (a life-threatening condition where your body temperature drops due to rapid cooling) is not something we worry about except in extreme elevations (and we aren't due for that until New Hampshire), we decide to let the rain have its way and enjoy nature's shower.

Gear is another story. You must protect your clothes and sleeping bag. Back in Virginia, I experienced the ponding of water in the bottom of my pack that saturated my gear. I didn't realize that a pack cover can also funnel rainwater to the bottom of the cover. You set the pack down and, presto, the puddle soaks your pack. By now I'm a bit wiser to the issue and stop to empty the bottom of the pack cover if the weather warrants it. And so far in Connecticut, we've had our share of rain.

Now the Fourth of July looks to be another wet and dreary day. We're not sad, however. As timing would have it, we're planning to stay with friends of Steve's near the town of Kent. Kent is a vacation hotspot for people fleeing the stone cities of Hartford and New York. There's lots of money here with nice homes set beside picturesque lakes. A great place to take a breather and enjoy a holiday. But clouds are rapidly lowering and rain soon splatters the windows of the van where just moments ago, we were picked up at a road crossing by Steve's friend.

I must say, I'm so relieved not to be hiking in the rain, I can hardly contain my joy. To me, a warm home and no rain is a great vacation. I happily do up the laundry, take a relaxing shower, and bask in the comfort of real furniture. Watching the rivulets of water running down the windowpanes, I think about what I take for granted back home. A warm, clean, comfortable home, safe from the storm. A comfy bed, clean clothes, and plenty to eat. It's interesting how much things like this come to mean to a tired and dirty hiker. Comparing each existence, a bed on the trail is a narrow sleeping bag and pad resting on the hard ground. Home is the backpack. Clothes are usually muddy and smelly. You're also the following:

- cold or hot (no in between)
- hungry and/or thirsty (almost always)
- tired and achy (usually)
- discouraged or elated (goes with the territory)

The Appalachian Trail can transport one to a third-world status of sorts, like what I experienced back in Overmountain Shelter when we ran out of food. It awakens a soul deadened by the pleasures of living in the United States. We should rise each day with thankful hearts for all that we possess here in a land of plenty. Looking back on my journey when I read this account of my travel, I'm reminded how trail life can be a catalyst to a thankful heart.

If only I could convince the family who has taken us in here in Kent how heavenly a safe haven can be. They are not in my walking shoes. In fact, they are downright upset that their plans for a picnic and fireworks have been skewed. I feel a little guilty for their misery while I'm as happy as a clam. I feel like I should be unhappy too. If only they knew what life is like on a rainy day trailside.

That evening the friends ask some relatives to stop by for a visit. For dessert they plan to serve brownie sundaes. I can't keep my mind off that scrumptious fact, even as I try to concentrate on one of the visitors—a young teen eager to hear all about our trip. She's fifteen and has plans to hike the Appalachian Trail one day. I'm ecstatic as I love sharing about our adventure. To a young, wide-eyed teen, eager to learn, I delve into the many aspects of our journey, from the interesting to the challenging. Nor am I shy either when it comes to acknowledging my need for God on this hike. It's the only way I've been able to come this far on the trail. I tell it like it is.

In the midst of sharing, we are presented with a brownie cradling a scoop of vanilla ice cream, decorated with chocolate syrup and whipped cream. If this isn't a vision of heaven after the descriptions of heaven in the midst of trail stories, I don't know what is. When the teen leaves that night, I have to wonder if, like me, she will see her dream realized when the time is right. I hope she'll let me know someday. I can plant, another waters, but God causes the growth, topped off by a delicious fudge brownie sundae.

The next morning we depart the town of Kent, blessed beyond measure by a place of refuge. Now it's time to hit the trenches of traildom—the mud, the hunger, the pain, the dream steadily coming to pass. I've heard it said Connecticut is easy terrain. Maybe it is, but with the high humidity left over from the previous day's rain, coupled with the heat, the going is tough. Steve falls far behind. I worry something might have happened to him and decide to wait for him at the next ridge. This is new for me compared to the hike we did in Virginia. I don't fuss or fume over how slow he is. I don't think of this as my little ol' hike. This is a team effort right now, so long as Steve is with us, and even when he is not physically there. One can't succeed without the other. Team work—it's what marriage is all about.

While I wait on a rocky outcropping for him to appear, I dry out the pack cover from the dripping vegetation that sometimes rains down for hours, even after a storm has passed. When Steve arrives, he's very glad to see me and a bit surprised as well. Soon after I realize there are benefits to casting aside my cares and allowing patience to reign instead. Such as the descent from the ridge we have just climbed. It's a series of rock-strewn boulders, slippery from the rain. Immediately the nagging fear of falling comes over me. I fuss and fume over the unexpected harshness. My aggravation at trying to clamber down off this ridge matches the terrain. Suddenly my foot slips. I'm heading over the rocks to an unknown fate. Instinctively Steve grabs hold of my backpack at the last second, keeping me from careening off the ledge in what would have been a disastrous spill. It's like a scene of danger set in slow motion. I don't even want to consider what might have happened. But when it turns out all right, onward you go. It's reminiscent of the many scenarios on this hike that could have ended in disaster. Chalk it up to divine intervention and the strength found in partnership.

Out of the cooler mountains, we now traverse the flatlands where the temperatures soar. Steve stares longingly at the Housatonic River skirting the trail. I know what that gleam in his eye means. Have water, will swim. While people stand along the river's edge fishing, Steve peels off his backpack, drop his kilt (but leaves on the underwear) and jumps in for a dip. I watch him, wondering what kind of bacteria might be lurking in there, but he is enjoying it too much. In Steve's mind, there's more to trail life than just walking. There's the "stopping to smell the roses" part. Honestly I haven't done much smelling on this hike. I recall one day down in southern Virginia when I forced myself to stop, sit down, and look at the clouds drifting overhead in some heavenly parade. For a time I was transported away from the duty of hiking to savor creation. But I have to force myself to do things like that. It's not a part of my nature.

Steve, on the other hand, doesn't need to make a schedule to enjoy a fine moment. This is why he hikes, to be a part of creation, not an invader. If I'm not forcing him to do miles, that is. He savors a dip in the muddy Housatonic River on a humid summer's day while I relax on the bank and try not to think about the miles we still need to make. Steve the rose sniffer, and me the goal setter.

When he finally emerges, refreshed from the dip, we continue on. The weather starts to deteriorate. By the time we reach the road crossing, heavy rain is falling. The stream before us is now a raging river from the July Fourth deluge and this afternoon's contribution. We elect to take the high water route which I immediately regret. It adds an extra mile of a useless PUD when we're already spent. I arrive first at the muddy campsite to find mosquitoes out for blood. I move quickly to throw on a head net and choose a place to set up the tent. Everywhere I look there's mud from all the precipitation. When I finally settle on a place to pitch the tent, Steve shows up and promptly collapses on the ground in exhaustion. For the first time, I do all the chores of putting up the tent and cooking dinner. I move quickly as I hear the sound of distant thunder. I fix dinner and urge him to eat. By the time we have everything done, the rain begins once more, and we scurry into our tent. Storms last all night long. I knew there would be times like this with rainy days and rainy nights. Par for the course. But our gear is now fairly soaked, and we hope the sun might at least peek out of the clouds so we can dry out.

The dawn of a new day also marks a new beginning for Paul Bunyan. We made the decision awhile back, when Steve joined in our hike, that we would allow our son the chance to strike out on his own for a few days. He would go the miles he wants, camp where he wants, cook and sleep on his schedule. At first I'm not happy about the plan. Motherly instinct, I suppose. We give him strict orders that once he gets to camp, he's to call us on his cell phone.

But even that doesn't settle my apprehension that's further magnified when I spy Paul Bunyan's pack cover still hanging from a tree that morning, forgotten in the wake of his hasty departure. Not a good way to start, especially with the recent rains we've been having. Visions fill my mind of Paul Bunyan's pack and its contents getting soaked. He could get chilled and sick or worse. There's little Steve and I can do though, even as we try to make time. We'd love to catch up to him on a mountain summit where he might be taking a snooze and give him the pack cover. For all the times he's fallen behind in the past, he remains a good half mile to a mile ahead of us. We're forced to leave his wellbeing in God's capable hands, again submitting to this all-too familiar test of faith.

I arrive on the summit of the next mountain to see a bank of dark clouds rolling our way. A doozy of a thunderstorm is fast approaching. We speed down toward the town of Falls Village, serenaded by the ominous sound of thunder, and take refuge under the front portico of a high school. As I watch the skies open up, I think of Paul Bunyan out there without his pack cover. I begin to pace, wondering where he is and if he's found safety from this rainy mess. When the weather clears, we pack up and head out as water still drips from saturated trees. I hope beyond hope that he's made it to the next scheduled shelter where we will be reunited.

No such luck. We arrive at the shelter to find he isn't there. Nor has he checked in via the cell phone. We have no idea where he is.

I try to cast my care on God, for He cares for us. I reach out in prayer for protection, that Paul Bunyan has found rest and warmth even if his gear is soaked. I especially pray that somehow we're going to meet up again.

How and when, I don't know. It's out of my hands.

CHAPTER TWELVE

NO PAIN, NO MAINE

MASSACHUSETTS

"For we walk by faith (we regulate our lives and conduct ourselves by our conviction or belief respecting man's relationship to God and divine nature, with trust and holy fervor, thus we walk) not by sight or appearance."

~ 2 Corinthians 5:7

Have you ever read the passage "walk by faith, not by sight" and wondered what it truly means? I've been walking this trail for months using my eyesight so as not to trip over a rock or root. I look for ticks and poison ivy. I rely on my eyes as a warning of potential danger. But I've also come to places on the trail where one can't use eyes to help in a crisis. Like on day two of this hike when my glasses broke. Or Overmountain Shelter when we ran out of food. I had to reach out with faith-filled eyes to places I could not see, to those with merciful hearts to help a hiker in need. I had to reach out in blind faith when I lay in some hospital bed in Pennsylvania, thinking I had a heart issue, to a place of grace when I thought I could hitch for a ride in New Jersey (only to discover later it was illegal) and have other hikers find rides for me instead.

Now I'm in another place of reaching out in faith concerning Paul Bunyan's circumstances. I spend a restless night in my tent, battling yet another rainy night (Connecticut has been filled with rainy days and nights) wondering how he's doing with his soggy gear. Where he spent the night. If he was warm enough. At least the danger of hypothermia this time of year is low. Still, the anxious mother in me wonders.

I pack up my gear and, along with Steve, trek on toward the town of Salisbury. We hope to inquire of the postmaster if a scraggly sixteen year old stopped by to pick up his mail drop. I'm still holding out hope that we'll cross paths with him. One never knows. It's a walk by faith, not by sight, isn't it?

Once in town we trudge along the bricked walkways, trying hard not to think about the various vacationers staring at two muddy, wet, disheveled hikers. We then spy a lone hiker heading toward us, sipping hot tea from a huge Styrofoam cup. It's none other than Paul Bunyan.

My heart leaps. Words cannot express my jubilation at seeing him healthy and happy. We have a joyful reunion there in the town square. While we dry out gear on the stone paths and walls, he relates his tale of the trail. How he arrived around 5 p.m. in Salisbury, wet and hungry, wandering around in search of food and companionship. Wondering, too, where he would spend the night. Finding a small grove of pine trees outside of town to pitch his little green tent away from the curious. Hoping, hoping to get some kind of signal on his cell phone so he could let us know he's okay. Ending with tears of frustration when he could not get ahold of us and spends a wet, drippy night in his little tent. Awakening this morning to find his hiking boots full of slugs and his heart feeling even worse. Returning to town in the hopes of seeing us as we came in to get our mail drop.

So what does he think about being out on his own, experiencing his first solo trail adventure?

JOSHUA

Aaaagh! What am I doing here?
Those are the thoughts running through my mind the first night on my own. I know everyone says doing the trail your way is the best way. But when you've been out with another person for so many months, it's probably not the best idea to separate. I learned that the hard way.

Before I went off on my own, my parents gave me instructions to call and let them know how I'm doing. Once I set up my stealth campsite in a pine forest about fifty feet from the trail, I came to realize a horrible fact. Salisbury has no cell coverage. Well, great. Now I need to trek the mile back into town and figure out how to call while finding food, as I'm pretty hungry.

If it had been in any other state, it might have been better. But Connecticut, specifically Salisbury, is not the friendliest place to be. I've been in plenty of trail towns where people say hello. These people don't.

I also distinctly remember hearing a little girl tell her mom, "Mommy, that boy smells. What's he doing here?" Kind of gives one an interesting look on the other side when comparing this encounter to a normal trail town and people used to smelly and dirty hikers.

Thankfully Salisbury has a grocery store where I buy a liter of soda, bread, and cheese for my dinner. After dinner I try to find a phone. I start walking, walking, walking. Apparently Salisbury has no payphones either. Finally I discover a phone at a governmental office building. I walk over but all that's left is the empty metal shelf where the payphone used to be. Despair begins to set in. I'm truly alone.

I head back to camp, hoping I will somehow get phone service. Miracle of miracles I get one bar on my cell phone while sitting in front of my tent. I make a call to my grandfather and tell him I'm okay. It's the best I can do.

All I can say is, if you decide to go off alone, make sure you're prepared for it. It's not as easy as it sounds.

LAURALEE

After our reunion, Paul Bunyan declares, "Well, I think I'll hang out with you guys after all." He's had enough of playing Lone Ranger. Even if we are the parents, at least we're people to talk to and share the trip with. And maybe, just maybe, we aren't too bad to hang out with. For me, I'm simply glad to have him back, safe and sound.

We're ready to continue the hike north. It isn't long before we reach the Massachusetts line. Connecticut has been an interesting and difficult ride for me. Contending with the enemies of heat, humidity, daily rains, Paul Bunyan's escapade, and the challenging terrain gives me a whole different outlook on the state. Entering Massachusetts is a welcome relief. Another state down, four to go. Only a little while ago I was standing on Springer Mountain with fourteen states to master. But make no mistake, the toughest terrain of the trail still awaits us.

For now Massachusetts hits us with unique challenges. It's not so much the terrain that tests us but the bugs who think we're the ultimate buffet. When the trail drops to a lower elevation and meanders by swamps and a river, mosquitoes thrive in abundance. We are irresistible appetizers waltzing through their domain. Slathering on the DEET, we try to outrun the swarms buzzing in our direction, ravenous in their quest. If you dare miss a spot, a mosquito will undoubtedly find it. The tip of an elbow, the back of your neck, the top of your lip, even the earlobe. It's also necessary to use a head net at times and sleep in a tent rather than inside the trail shelters. There are even shelters listed in the guidebooks that speak of the bug problems and to avoid these areas if possible. Inside my tent, I see mosquitoes clinging to the no-see-um netting, eager for a bite as soon as I emerge and before the DEET can be applied. It's crazy stuff.

But there are other challenges besides mosquitoes. One night we elect to escape the infested campsites and stay at a quaint inn. That morning at the inn, Paul Bunyan inadvertently steps on the buckle to the waist belt of my backpack, breaking off a tong. I can still fasten the belt, so I figure everything is okay.

It isn't. The day starts out hot and humid. The mosquitoes are ferocious. Paul Bunyan is barely making it (he is not a heat and humidity person). At one point he decides he's not taking another step and sits down in the shade to think things through. To make matters worse, my waist belt is slipping from the broken buckle and won't hold. Without a waist belt, I can't carry my backpack.

At a road junction, the decision becomes clear. I must get off the trail and get the buckle repaired. We talk about our situation and decide to have Steve's father come get us at Great Barrington. Since we're in Massachusetts and Steve's parents live near Albany, New York, it's not too far of a journey. We can also get out of the oppressive heat. By now Paul Bunyan has caught up with us, and we tell him our plan. Steve asks a neighbor for a ride to the town of Great Barrington. In a matter of a few hours my father-in-law is picking us up for a quick retreat into the comforts of civilization.

Yes, there is a time to hike, but there is also a time to rest. And a time to sit in air-conditioned comfort, eat lots of food, delight in the fact you don't have to smell like eau de DEET, and get a backpack repaired. But the white blazes are calling. There's a job left to do. A dream to fulfill. Even if it's the height of summer and there will be plenty more humid, hot days and bugs ahead, it's time to go forth and conquer.

With our eyes fixed on the goal of Katahdin, my father-in-law drives us back to our starting point in Massachusetts.

We set out to conquer this rather narrow state. The weather cooperates with cooler temperatures as we lounge by a pond. I scoop out large quantities of Nutella—a delectable chocolate, hazelnut spread—and eat it by the spoonful. I'm taking a rare moment out of the hike to smell the roses and enjoy the beauty that God has made. It's not long before I'm attacking this trail once again. A moment is all I can spare, I fear.

At Upper Goose Pond, hikers are greeted by a large cabin with bunks to sleep in. I elect to set up my tent and enjoy a bit of respite. The cabin itself fills to capacity with college-aged hikers, all eager and chomping at the bit with news of their adventures. Paul Bunyan is happy to be with young people closer to his age. Energized by a delicious pancake breakfast the following morning, courtesy of the head caretaker, we're ready to accomplish another goal of mine—crossing the Massachusetts Turnpike. I recall as a young girl traveling the turnpike many times, keeping my eyes peeled for the bridge where the trail crosses, heralded by a large sign that reads APPALACHIAN TRAIL. I once daydreamed of some long-distance hike. Now the dream is being fulfilled.

I pause in the middle of the bridge that overlooks cars and trucks whizzing by at great speed. So, too, the years have whizzed by, bringing me to this point in time that I've pondered for so long. Years are like days. It may seem long, but it really isn't. In a twinkling of an eye it can become reality. I'm here just as I imagined I would be. The moment goes beyond what I could have hoped or dreamed.

Steve snaps a picture of me on my dream bridge, and we hike on, stopping momentarily to fetch some cold drinks and snacks out of a cooler left by some generous trail angels (more about these wondrous people in the next chapter). By afternoon we reach a trail crossing and a road that leads to the Cookie Lady—another generous trail angel who gives out homemade cookies to hungry hikers. We find her husband taking over the role, dubbed Cookie Man, who presents us each with a homemade oatmeal raisin cookie. I munch away, thinking what a nice day this is turning out to be.

I march along, confident and sure. We pass trail maintainers working to keep the trails clear of overgrowth. Fresh leaves color the trail green. Life is good.

Suddenly my foot gives way. I slide down the trail, wrenching my right ankle in the process. It's a sickening pain. I know I've just suffered a severe ankle sprain.

Shake it off, it will be okay. I think about the other times God relieved the pain. Helped my aches. Healed my wounds. It's been such a good day, it can't end like this.

By the time I reach the next road crossing, I can barely walk. I sit down and try to decide what to do. A fellow hiker gives me an elastic bandage, which I use to secure my ankle. I try walking on it, hoping it has the strength to make it to the next shelter where we plan to meet Paul Bunyan. But it's too painful to walk. Having suffered an ankle injury a few years ago, I know I need ice and rest.

With a heavy heart and tear-filled eyes, I tell Steve that I need to leave the trail. As we contemplate our dilemma, a truck pulls up. A day hiker exits, carrying a brand new camera. We tell him about my injury and ask about facilities in the nearby town of Pittsfield. He pauses, looks at his new camera he'd wanted to test on a short day hike, then waves us over to his truck. He drives us to town and then on to his own home where his wife gives me an ice pack for my ankle and treats us to crackers and Brie cheese. I'm overwhelmed by their hospitality. But with the ankle swelling and bruising, it's plain to see I need to let this heal rather than try to go on. We call my father-in-law once more to come pick us up.

While Steve and the day hiker return to fetch Paul Bunyan out of the woods, I talk to the woman about my hike and the Christian books I write. She tells me she's a Christian, too. I'm glad to hear this with my heart burdened by what has happened. The disappointment hurts as much as my ankle. After such a wonderful day, it's hard to see it end like this.

Now I'm back at my in-laws where I'd only left two days ago. There I make an executive decision. I need time to recuperate and recondition the ankle if I have any hope of finishing the trail this year. That means heading home to Virginia. It's a tough call, especially for Steve who wanted to hike with us to Vermont. We'd planned for him to enjoy New England, and now it won't happen. As for me, I only pray there's enough time to heal and return to finish the trail.

It seems strange, leaving our hike and heading back to familiar territory. I fight the notion that I surrendered to a simple injury. But in the back of my mind lurks the toughest section of the trail. Many say that 90% of the work remains when one enters the New England states, especially the White Mountains of New Hampshire. How can I possibly make it through that kind of terrain if I'm not in good physical condition?

There's something to be said about how previous trials prepare us for future events. Like nursing an ankle sprain. I know how to do this from my last bout with a devastating ankle injury several years ago. Back then, the sports doctor said I'd never hike again. Well, guess what? I'm hiking, and I plan to return to this hike as soon as possible. Once home I begin ice massaging. Performing sets of exercises on the affected ankle. Wrapping it in an elastic bandage and keeping it elevated. Learning patience with the healing process. Giving the limb time to rest but also balancing it with exercises to get it moving again.

A week passes. I can tell Steve's heart is wandering as he's supposed to be on the trail and not stuck at home. I want to do something for him; something he will enjoy. Trail life had been tough on him. The ascents and descents, the thunderstorms and biting bugs, dealing with an injured wife—it's worn him out.

Then an idea comes to me. We'll head to the beach for a few days. Steve can swim and boat to his heart's content. When I suggest it, he's dubious of the plan. Will it jeopardize my recovery? I feel I'm well enough to make the trip.

So off we go to the Outer Banks of North Carolina for sand, ocean waves, swimming, and eating. A far cry from trail life these last few months. My ankle is sensitive and weak, but I hobble around as best I can. Steve goes sailing with Paul Bunyan. I'm able to play several rounds of miniature golf. We head down the beach for a trip to see the ocean waves and feel the golden sand under our feet.

I feel better about things after we return. Especially now that the trail itch is starting up in earnest, as the days trickle down one by one on the calendar. Nearly two weeks have gone by. I still walk with a limp, but I'm determined to return to the trail. It will be tough to say the least, even with hiking poles and an ankle brace. But time is running out. It's now or never.

A reluctant Steve gives his blessing on our departure. I'm really going out on a limb now, especially with the most difficult part of trail yet to go. Paul Bunyan and I say good-bye to Steve, gather up the gear, and head to the car for the long nine-hour trip back to my in-laws. I vow not to stop the hike again unless I break something. This is the final frontier. The last effort. There can be no more injuries. No more weather breaks. *No rain, no pain, no Maine.* I must hike on to the end, walking by faith, not by sight. Or I will return home in defeat.

CHAPTER THIRTEEN

TRAIL ANGELS AND OTHER WONDROUS HIKER BEINGS

VERMONT

"Alone we can do so little; together we can do so much."

~ Helen Keller

I remember long ago how I wanted to see a real angel. I read, of course, about the angelic encounters experienced by the biblical personages like Abraham, Daniel, and Mary. They were eyewitnesses to heavenly beings that shared good news and displayed great might. There's been television series where angels help humans overcome their challenges. Once, long ago, I asked to see an angel. I must admit, I was a tad apprehensive. What if this tall, glimmering figure showed up in my room, arms outstretched, ready to issue some divine decree? But curiosity outweighed nerves. I wanted to see something extraordinary.

Suddenly I heard this tingling like the sound of a bell. I headed for the bedroom. My lampshade was shaking. Just the lampshade. Nothing else. Could it be?

"Okay, okay, I've seen enough!" I called out before something really *did* materialize.

The Bible speaks of entertaining angels unaware. Like the

person who shows up at the front doorstep asking for help. Or the three angels who visit a subdued Abraham and give him words of encouragement. On the Appalachian Trail, angels have already surrounded Paul Bunyan and me in various ways. I'm sure they're working overtime to keep us from the dangers inherent while hiking the trail.

Out here there are also trail angels—people of true mercy who go out of their way to help hikers. They are wondrous folks doing extraordinary things right here on earth and never expecting anything in return.

Fortunately I already had the privilege of encountering angels of mercy. Like at Overmountain Shelter where hiker angels offered food to a starving mom and her son. Or goodies like sodas and snacks that trail angels left at road intersections. Or those who came one evening to a lowly shelter, bringing us bread and fruit. Or who intervene with prayer and kind words via the e-mails I receive while in town. And then there are the town angels encountered through the trail experience. Like when I injured my ankle and the man drove us to his home where his wife dutifully cared for me. All of them are true angels of the heart and soul.

As I begin the next section of trail, I always wonder what awaits me—in the terrain, in the testing of my physical ability, and in the people I will meet. That first day back on the trail after my ankle injury, we enter the town of Dalton, Massachusetts, to meet two friendly guys hiking the entire trail. Their trail names are Sherlock and Circuit Rider, and they've done this trail thing before. In fact they are on a second 2,000-mile wander. I sometimes envy a hiker who has a no-nonsense, peaceful way of encountering the unknown. Like these two guys who radiate confidence everywhere they go. We chat and move on. I know we'll never see one another again as they'll breeze by in short order. But you never know.

Paul Bunyan and I now climb the highest peak in

Massachusetts, Mount Greylock. It soon becomes obvious that the two-week hiatus off the trail has weakened our once top-notch hiker strength. We're dragging from the physical challenge. Paul Bunyan falls behind. I plan a motel night to get us back into the swing of things. I arrive at a trail intersection about two miles shy of the motel and decide to wait for Paul Bunyan to arrive. It's only 3:30 in the afternoon. Plenty of time to head down the mountain and have a leisurely evening. I sit and wait.

I wait. And wait some more.

It's now 5 p.m. He couldn't be *that* far behind. When it reaches 5:30, I panic. We've only been on the trail two days, and Paul Bunyan is already missing. I throw on my pack, realizing I'm going to have to hike back up the mountain and look for him. I'm already tired, but I have no choice.

About halfway up the mountain, I encounter Sherlock and Circuit Rider. "Oh, we saw Paul Bunyan and hiked with him for a time. He's maybe a half hour behind."

I'm glad they've seen him but I wonder why he's so far back. When he finally appears, I discover he's had a bout with stomach issues all day. We only make it to shelter that night rather than the motel, but I'm glad he's safe. Two hikers watched over him and encouraged him. They were momentary hiker angels in our time of need.

The next day I stop at a store to buy Paul Bunyan some medicine and food. We now cross into Vermont, our third to the last state. Hard to believe. Every day I draw closer to finishing the Appalachian Trail. I've seen small goals come and go. Making it through the Smokies. Entering my home state of Virginia. Heading north of the Mason Dixon line. Seeing the cliffs of Delaware Water Gap where I used to camp as a child. Coming to the bridge spanning the Massachusetts Turnpike where I once pondered if I'd ever do a long-distance hike. Now I've hit another state, and like every day on this journey, I wonder what lies ahead.

I read in my trail guide that Vermont is home to ski resorts, beaver ponds, and a place where the Appalachian Trail shares a hundred miles with its sister trail called, appropriately, The Long Trail. But on this particular day it's the water situation that concerns me. Many of the water sources are polluted by beaver activity. Avoiding sources that can spawn giardia or beaver fever—a waterborne illness from an amoeba—is important. It can cause diarrhea for weeks. My water treatment so far on the trip has been chemicals in the form of chlorine dioxide to help kill microorganisms. But I don't feel safe using just chemicals on this part of the trail with beaver dams everywhere.

Unfortunately the only other source of water for miles is a mud pit. For the next three hours I hike without water. Temperatures soar into the 80s. I've never experienced true thirst like I do now, and it's not a pleasant experience. It becomes a driving force for me to seek water, to have that cool liquid run over a parched and scratchy throat. It's like oil running over the dry areas of life, bringing healing. It revives. It makes you whole again and gives you the ability to go on. And when you don't have it, the need for it consumes you.

By the time I stumble to the shelter, my thirst is overwhelming. I see an older lady standing by the creek, using a hand pump to rid the water of nasty microorganisms. I look at the bounty of fresh water she has treated with her water pump and promptly tell her what has transpired over the last few hours. Immediately she offers me the use of her water pump so I can have fresh water right away. I gladly accept, and in a matter of minutes I'm drinking all that I can while enjoying what I craved for miles. She's another hiker angel to the rescue.

I find a kindred spirit in the older woman who calls herself Signage. (She likes to look for signs that inform her of mileage points on the trail, hence her trail name.) At this point, I've had no contact with any women my age since the

Smokies with Hikernutt. Signage is refreshing, and she seems pleased to have found another female soul tackling this trail. She tells of a good friend of hers who got off unexpectedly in Massachusetts and how she's been hiking solo. I wonder if we're destined to do a good chunk of the trail together. She tells me she's meeting a friend in two days who plans to drive her into the town of Manchester Center for a dental appointment. Paul Bunyan and I are welcome to tag along if we want to resupply and have some fun. I hadn't thought that far in advance, but here an angel in disguise has done the thinking for me by providing a means of transportation into town. I eagerly accept.

We hike on through the pleasant Vermont woods. When we reach the shelter that night, it's overflowing with would-be hikers looking to complete The Long Trail. Campsites are few, and I'm finding myself on edge. Once again Signage comes to the rescue. She gives me the one good spot left to pitch a tent while she erects hers in a literal hole in the ground. It's hard to truly appreciate the impact of such kindness in the heat of the moment and when you're tired. It's easy to recall the bad but not the blessings that are given over and beyond what we could ask or think. I'm glad I'm keeping a written journal of my hikes where I jot down where I've been and what has occurred. Looking back at them now, the words are worth their weight in gold.

While we are camping at the shelter area, Paul Bunyan elects to spend the night on top of Glastenbury Mountain in the fire tower. There he captures both the sunrise and sunset on our camera, one of the few times we are able to take pictures of each. There is something good about seeing the rising and setting of the sun. It speaks of constancy and faithfulness. The trail brings to mind the fulfillment of many biblical principles I once half-heartedly considered. Not everyone can do a long-distance hike like the Appalachian Trail, but we can recall times in our lives where the words we see and hear come to life and things happen. They are not just ancient verses for another era but are appropriate for today and in every circumstance.

At the next road crossing, I meet another trail angel here on earth by way of Signage's friend, Mary Anne. I'm already impressed by the things Signage has shared regarding this woman. Talk about a true friend above friends. Mary Anne is here, all the way from the outskirts of Washington, D. C., to take Signage to the dentist in Manchester Center. Driving from Maryland to Vermont for a friend's dental appointment. How's that for true friendship?

Despite the long drive, Mary Anne cheerfully picks up us grungy hikers and transports us to town. We are barely settled in the car when she reveals all the goodies she has tucked away in plastic tubs, along with cold drinks in an ice chest. It's like heaven on earth.

The following day, Mary Anne turns into a regular taxicab service while we run errands in town. She picks us up at the hostel, takes us to a restaurant for breakfast, onward to the laundromat with all our dirty stuff, to the post office and finally all the way back to the trailhead. But the kindness is not over. At the parking lot she insists on loading us up with food. We have sandwich bags filled with pepperoni and cheese, crackers, and Snicker bars. My little pouch hanging from my waist belt is nearly bursting from all the goodies. It's going to be a very nice lunch at the summit of Stratton Mountain, courtesy of trail angel Mary Anne.

I hope to see Signage again after the few days we spent together, but it's not to be. We each end up going different paces on the trail. I'll miss her, but I'm thankful for the few short days we did spend together and especially for the kindness of her friend, who went over and beyond the call of duty.

Vermont is turning out to be a beautiful and interesting state as we ascend the ski mountains to splendid views of the

Green Mountains. At times the trail follows major ski paths down the mountainside. But on one section of the trail, I trip over a root and fall forward, using my left hand to brace the impact. The pain is intense. I've bruised the hand quite badly, I can tell, so much so that I can't even hold my hiking pole.

I fear the worst. I vowed back in Massachusetts I would not get off the trail again unless I did something major, like bust a bone. I quickly pray this is not the case, even as the hand begins to swell. How I wish I had ice to calm the inflammation. Where is one supposed to find ice on the trail in the middle of summer unless it's in a town? I do find a trickling stream to cool my bruised flesh, but again I'm forced to trust in the unseen and not in my situation.

Heading downhill to a road crossing, I spy something white sitting on the trail. It's a Styrofoam ice chest left by another trail angel. I've seen such ice chests before, some of which contain cold drinks and best of all, ice. Hoping for a miracle, I open it to discover beer. And nestled around those beer cans are bags of ice! Immediately I take out a Ziploc bag, dump ice into it and apply it to my bruised hand. To whomever the angel of mercy was who left that miracle of ice, it likely saved my injured hand and perhaps even my hike.

Just then Paul Bunyan catches up to me, panting heavily. He heard through the hiker grapevine that I'd taken a fall and severely injured my hand. (I had mentioned it earlier to a passing hiker heading in the opposite direction.) I'm surprised to see him, as usually he takes his time on any given day, keeping to his own schedule. But when he found out Mom was hurt, he hightailed it down off the mountain.

Now he thrusts something in my direction. "Here. I found this lying beside the trail. I thought maybe you could use it."

It's a two-inch-wide elastic wrap, still sealed in plastic and exactly the right size to support my injured hand.

My mouth falls open. *Wow.*

I take stock in what I've been given. I have ice. I have a

bandage. I have confidence. And all presented to me on some wilderness trail where things like this are never available. Coincidence? You be the judge. But all I can say is my doubts have taken flight. The answer on this hike is an unequivocal *yes* and *amen*. I matter. The hike matters, too.

Our next rest stop on the trail is the junction of Route 4 at a place called Mendon Lodge. I send Paul Bunyan ahead to pick up our mail drop and find us a place to stay. When I arrive, he's all smiles. The lady at the lodge has left the buffet breakfast set up just for me, despite it being long past the time to close. I call Steve to tell him where we are and what has happened the last few days. I also tell him of a slight equipment malfunction I've been experiencing—my sleeping pad is leaking. He offers little in the way of suggestions on the phone. An hour later the phone rings and it's my in-laws. They are on their way from Albany, New York, to take me to Rutland to see about getting another pad.

Yet another *wow* of the hike.

When my in-laws arrive, it's like having a taste of home greeting us on the trail. They take us to Rutland and the outfitters where I find a temporary replacement for my mattress. They treat us to a special lunch at a restaurant. What a great time of refreshing with a touch of love and interest that makes one hike on and enjoy the journey.

Which is good, because the tough stuff still awaits us. I steady myself as we cross the Connecticut River into New Hampshire after being treated to roadside blessings by trail angels who leave homemade chocolate chip cookies and a vase filled with flowers. I'm in awe over what's happened. But so much more awaits Paul Bunyan and me—including the most difficult test to come.

The White Mountains of New Hampshire.

Chapter Fourteen

The Agony and the Ecstasy

New Hampshire

"Forewarned, forearmed;
to be prepared is half the victory."

~ Miguel de Cervantes, Spanish novelist

There is an old saying, *forewarned is forearmed*. If anything, the White Mountains of New Hampshire is a place where one must be warned so one can be armed with insight and wise decision-making. This is some of the most rugged, wild, arduous but beautiful places the Appalachian Trail has to offer. In one section alone the trail runs fourteen miles above tree line on the mountain summit, at the mercy of every storm and blast of wind. Not to mention the terrain itself—steep, rocky, and tough on limb and mental faculty. I tasted some of this terrain early on during other family hiking trips. We faced bad weather and hypothermia, aching limbs and spectacular scenery. But it's a completely different scenario when you're doing this terrain with a loaded backpack, accompanied by your son, with just a few weeks of the hike remaining until the end.

Now my concern for the "Whites"—as they are called in

hiking circles—increases from roaming butterflies in the pit of my stomach to genuine fear. I'm literally a nervous wreck the morning I awake at the Hiker's Welcome Hostel in Glencliff, New Hampshire. This is the day we're scheduled to climb our first mountain above the tree line, Mount Moosilauke. Some say it's extremely treacherous, especially in rain. I imagine another twisted ankle or other injury that takes me off the trail permanently. Maybe being forewarned can also lead to irrational fear. The fear becomes so great that I literally heave, wondering how I will ever do this section. The agony has begun, and I have yet to place a foot on the trail within the borders of the Whites.

But God is faithful to meet me in my place of weakness. We begin packing up that morning. As we do, I overhear another hiker planning to take a shuttle and slackpack Moosilauke (that is, just take a daypack for the trip). She plans on hiking north to south, the easier way to handle this type of terrain. Suddenly my wheels begin turning. I wonder if we could split the cost of the shuttle and do the same hike. At least it would alleviate some of my anxiety and ensure us a warm place to spend the night. I inquire, and the plan is set into motion.

We climb our first mountain above tree line in foggy, windy weather. There are no views at the summit of Moosilauke, only a strong wind that buffets us. On the way down, the skies open and rain soaks me from head to foot. At least I have a place of refuge at the hostel with a roof over my head. When I arrive back, Paul Bunyan is already there, gleefully telling me how he escaped the rain. No matter. I'm thankful to be safe and sound, having completed the first mountain of the Whites. I'm feeling more confident that we will be able to navigate this unpredictable section of trail.

The next day of hiking involves the notorious Kinsmans, of which I have heard of slick rock faces and the need to haul oneself up the rocks using feet and hands. I inhale a deep breath, summoning courage and not the fear that nearly paralyzed me yesterday. It helps that we awake to a picture-perfect day for the ascent. But I inform Paul Bunyan we need to stick together in the Whites. This is not without reason. We already had our time in these mountains a few years back when Paul Bunyan suffered a bout of hypothermia in the Presidential Range. I'd never seen the effects of hypothermia until I witnessed his entire demeanor change. He became obstinate. Disoriented. I didn't know what to think. Until we got him into warm, dry clothing, and he suddenly became rational again. After that scenario, never again would I take the mountains for granted. Nor would I jeopardize safety. Hypothermia is real.

So we stick together, for better or for worse. And the weather for the Kinsman section is extraordinary. We see the lofty peaks that await us in the Franconia Range. I do love the White Mountains, even for all their wicked weather and terrain. The adrenaline to succeed is clearly felt, especially having overcome the mental apprehension regarding Moosilauke and the Kinsmans.

On day three we begin our ascent to the Franconia Ridge via the Liberty Springs Trail. The weather has changed, as it often does in mountainous regions. Rain falls, and the wind picks up. Not the best weather for a hike above tree line, but that doesn't stop us. I've been on the Appalachian Trail a good four and a half months now, enduring just about everything. I can surely handle a little wind and rain.

That is, until I sense foreboding when I see a mass exodus of hikers coming down off the ridge on a Saturday morning. *What's up with that?* The action cries out *danger*. Does some unseen monster lurk at the summit or something?

We stop off at the caretaker's hut at Liberty Springs Tentsite to inquire about the conditions. I learn from the caretaker of the monster in the form of "zeros" up on the ridge—zero visibility and, to my alarm, zero degree wind chills. In August? Welcome to the White Mountains. He knew we were seasoned hikers and said we could probably do the ridge, but it wouldn't be a pretty walk. Standing there, clad in my T-shirt and shorts from the steep ascent, my son and I both starting to shiver, I know the decision that needs to be made. I have not forgotten the hypothermia incident. Despite it being only 10 a.m. and completing only two miles for the day, we decide to stay and wait for better weather.

We erect the tent in wind that gusts to near forty miles an hour. I'm still in my shorts and shivering like crazy. My fingers have lost all feeling. I feel clumsy. Hypothermia is closing in fast. We hastily get the tent up, change, and hunker down in sleeping bags. The rain and wind buffet our tent, but we are safe and warm in this bit of constructed heaven in the midst of a raging storm.

The next day dawns in heavy fog, but the rain has stopped. We pack up and head for the ridge. Clouds blanket the area. We see nothing but cold gray rocks ten feet ahead. We have no idea what the terrain we're hiking is like, even though I know the mountains of Little Haystack, Lincoln, and Lafayette exist somewhere in the fog. The wind pounds us, gusting to near sixty miles per hour. It throws us off our feet and slams us into nearby rocks and boulders. Paul Bunyan falls behind, and once more the hypothermia scenario of a few years ago returns to haunt me. I tell him he has to keep moving, and I make sure he's properly clothed. I talk to him frequently. We continue to move slowly and only when we stumble upon the signpost atop Lafayette do I have any idea where we are. By now we're exhausted, trying to move against a fierce tempest that pushes us backward. Though the White Mountains throw all its might in our direction, I refuse to yield to its cruel touch.

When we finally reach Mount Garfield, we look back to discover a clear Franconia Ridge from Lafayette all the way to Liberty. Not a single cloud graces the sky above. Though fog and wind had been our lot in life, the ridge is as peaceful as a new day.

I'm furious! I throw off my pack and hurl it to the ground. Why did we experience hell on the ridge while others can enjoy heaven amid unobstructed views in all directions? It's the way of the Whites, like a nasty playmate who plays tricks. Storms can blow in without provocation. The next hour it can afford views that extend to nearby states.

My seething doesn't last long. I shoulder my backpack and hike on. I will conquer this rugged mass of rock and boulder, no matter what it gives me in return.

After the situation on Franconia Ridge, it's clear I need to keep track of changing weather patterns. I don't relish facing another round of storminess in the next section, the Presidentials, with its fourteen continuous miles above the tree line. We check up on the weather whenever we pass through the AMC huts (dwellings built by the Appalachian Mountain Club that offer lodging and food to hikers for a hefty price), along with enjoying our fill of all the pancakes we can eat for a buck, left from breakfast. We use the work-for-stay option the huts offer to long-distance hikers like ourselves. This means arriving at the hut early enough to do a few hours of work for whatever leftovers remain from the evening meal, along with the privilege of bunking down on the floor of the hut's main dining area.

For our first work-for-stay experience at the Galehead Hut, Paul Bunyan and I are asked to speak to the overnight guests about our experience as a mother/son team hiking the Appalachian Trail. Normally I'm not a public speaker, but this proves to be an enjoyable task. We describe our journey and the gear we use to eager guests gathered around us. I see more and more how I'm doing things I've never done before. Could it be that new trails are being forged in the midst of a hike—like the trail to a future in public speaking?

At the hut, we discover the weather outlook in the Whites is favorable for the next few days. The Crawford Path, which the Appalachian Trail follows, affords stupendous views including the granddaddy of the section, Mount Washington. I enjoy the trail as it passes fragile alpine plants desperate to survive the harsh environment. I look at their resilience in fascination, wondering how these delicate plants can thrive with fierce wind and temperatures that dip to the arctic realms, not to mention the trampling of human feet that sometimes seek the easy way off the main trail. There's a lesson or two one can learn from that sheer will to exist despite life's harsh reality.

Arriving at the Lakes of the Clouds Hut, we again accept the work-for-stay option. Paul Bunyan's job is washing pots and pans bigger than he is. Mine is cleaning out the freezer in the cold basement of the hut. That night we're rewarded with the golden glow of a sunset over the same ridge that tried to overcome us a few days ago—the Franconia Ridge. I hope it's a sign of a glowing future and victory at the end of this stretch of trail. We are readying ourselves to hike the most rugged part yet, and I remain hopeful.

Hope is dashed in the middle of the night when I suddenly fall ill with a violent stomach flu. I spend most of the night hours awake in the rest room with stomach cramps. At 2 a.m., sick as a dog, I try desperately to get ahold of Steve. I figure it's useless. Cell phones don't work at this elevation. But I try anyway, and, to my amazement, his sleepy voice greets me! I relay to him my illness, and he in turn prays for me. But the next morning I find myself weak and groggy after only two hours of sleep. I face a mental sort of hell, trying to figure out what to do with the hike. The Presidential Range, fourteen continuous miles above tree line, is staring at me in all its rocky, harsh reality. I decide I should bail out for now by way of the Tuckerman Ravine Trail, to recover. I will do the Presidentials another time. It seems the only thing to do.

That morning I hear the weather report predicting one more clear day for hiking. The rest of the week will be dominated by rain and thunderstorms. If I'm going to do those fourteen miles above tree line and do it without any potential weather issues, it must be today, no matter how I feel. The ultimate challenge is now thrust before me. Can a difficult section be done on no sleep, no nutrition, and a half-sick body? Paul Bunyan would rather we bail out. He is no more interested in doing the Presidentials than I am. But like those delicate alpine plants that struggle to survive under the worst of conditions, to grow when it's most favorable (and that isn't often), I, too, must struggle to continue. It's now or never.

I struggle up the rocky hillside, one mile to the summit of Mount Washington. Once there we head into the cafeteria for a bite to eat. I'm able to keep down some yogurt, so things are looking up. We're also treated to views extending to the mountains of Maine and even the Atlantic Ocean—a rarity at that time of year, or so an employee tells me. It provides further incentive to go on, as weak as I am.

And go for it, I do. I take many breaks and eat simple carbohydrates to keep up my strength. I try to avoid anything heavy on my queasy stomach. I also take strength from two weary southbound hikers who talk of the hard terrain, which begs the question: Is this trail a relaxing and fun venture or bona fide hard work to achieve some monstrous goal?

Both, in all honesty.

The rocky scree fields on Jefferson and Adams chew up my feet and test my fortitude. Fortunately my strength slowly returns as I keep hiking. The weather holds with beautiful views all around. But I still have a difficult task left to finish the day—Mount Madison, with one of the severest descents on the trail. At that moment, I fall into company with another hiker who guides me down the trail of boulders like an angel in disguise. When she takes a side trail back to her car, I'm sorry to see her go. I like having a guide to help me negotiate the most difficult part of boulder hopping. Step by step, rock by rock, I make my way down the steep mountainside. When I arrive at Osgood Tentsite, Paul Bunyan has secured us a tent platform. I'm never more thankful to have completed this difficult section. Too exhausted to do much of anything, my son takes charge, setting up the tent and even cooking dinner. I collapse for the night, overcome by what I have done.

After that harrowing experience, we spend a day in the town of Gorham to recover. But we're back on the trail all the earlier the following day, courtesy of a lady who drives us thirteen miles to the trailhead. Up next is the Carter-Moriah Range of the Whites. Figuring I had already mastered the upside and downside of bouldering, I'm as ready as I'll ever be. But again the mountains push will and fortitude to the breaking point.

On North Carter, gazing down the slick, steep rocks that one must slide their way down with a loaded backpack, I decide I'm done with the whole show. I'm tired of the fear, thinking I might die or get hurt. I'm tired of trying to overcome this unforgiving terrain. I'm ready to hurl my backpack off the precipice, if not for Paul Bunyan who catches the pack strap. But then I take stock in what is happening. Will I allow the mountain to conquer me through my frustration? Or will I conquer it? I choose to channel the frustration into something positive. It's the mental shift I need to finish this tough section. We do and reward ourselves once more in the friendly town of Gorham for much needed R&R.

Didn't I say the trail through the White Mountains is both agony and ecstasy? Now they are complete. The hardest part is over. I can rest.

Not by a long shot.

CHAPTER FIFTEEN

BLOW OUT THE CANDLES

THE MAHOOSUCS OF MAINE

"There must be a day or two in a man's life when he is the
precise age for something important."
~ Franklin P. Adams

It's a bright and beautiful day. We feel refreshed, having
just spent two days basking in a nice motel room and the
pleasantries that inhabit town life. It all must come to an
end as the trail calls to us, only this time there's a certain
expectation in the air. We're heading toward the final state
on this long trek—Maine. For so long I have heard the catch-
all phrase in my head of "no pain, no rain, no Maine." We
definitely suffered pain on this journey. Had our share of
rain and snowstorms. Now Maine is about to materialize
before us in just a few short days.

We depart Gorham well rested, with full backpacks, ready
for whatever lies head. It's going to be a great time. I'm eager
to have my picture taken by the small blue sign that reads
poetically MAINE, THE WAY THINGS OUGHT TO BE. Who wouldn't,
having come nearly 2,000 miles of difficult treadway to
reach this point?

But like everything else in this journey, Maine is not so
easy to come by, even for a few days of hiking. In fact, it's

downright difficult. The terrain is steep and rocky with ladders and other challenges. Bog bridges that are supposed to keep us afloat sink in the mud. The weather taunts us with pending storms. I heard upon leaving Gorham of a front moving in that could spell rain for the toughest mile on the Appalachian Trail—Mahoosuc Notch—which boasts house-sized boulders and other obstacles. For many hikers, that one mile can take several hours, and it's definitely not a part I care to go through in a storm.

The toughest mile on the Appalachian Trail, Mahoosuc Notch in Maine

I need to pace myself. Heading toward the Maine state line is taking every ounce of fortitude with the relentless ups and downs. I'm slowly being worn away by the mental severity of this thing. I figured the Whites would be my toughest mental battle, but the trail heading toward that little blue Maine sign is wearing me down so much that popping Vitamin I (ibuprofen) doesn't begin to deal with the pain of achy limbs and a tired spirit.

When I finally do reach the little blue sign that says MAINE, THE WAY THINGS OUGHT TO BE, I'm less than thrilled. In fact,

I'm mad at what I have been through. But I also want my picture taken, so I ask a fellow hiker, Raindog, to take one on my camera while I summon some manner of a smile. I stand there in a sweaty shirt and dirty legs, wondering if this is the way things ought to be, as the sign says. Where is the exultation? Hey hiker babe...this is MAINE! Remember how far away Maine seemed back in Georgia? Like a far-off planet? You're in Maine. You hurt, yes, but those nasty looking legs have gotten you a long way.

The ecstasy I should be feeling is quickly squashed by further difficulty as we approach Mahoosuc Notch, followed by a steep climb up Mahoosuc Arm. I decide to devote an entire day to hiking both. We enter the notch on a warm, humid day but with an optimism to enjoy the challenge as much as humanly possible. We know it's tough from all the reports I have read, and it does not fail to please. It offers huge boulders, tight spaces, slick, dripping rock, even a dead moose rotting in the notch. Paul Bunyan helps me down slabs of slick rock courtesy of his famous walking stick that has been a part of his hiking repertoire since Damascus, Virginia. It now serves as a footrest to assist my descent. In certain places Paul Bunyan shuttles our packs through while we crawl on our hands and knees like spelunkers. This is the ultimate adventure, no doubt about it.

We take three hours to hike that one mile and make it out of the notch in one piece. I stop at a campsite to call Steve and give him the good news of surviving the trail's most difficult and notorious part. Now we have a steep climb up the Arm, and then we can rest. I'm happy even if the trip today is a measly five miles. Five whole miles when I used to hike eighteen miles or more. Arriving at Speck Pond that afternoon, five miles might as well have been eighteen with the intensity of it. And with storm clouds gathering on the horizon, I'm glad we're calling it quits for the day. It feels even better to be in a shelter, listening to the pounding of rain on the roof and watching other soggy hikers trudge in, knowing I'm safe and sound.

Still I seem to have a knack for entertaining false assumptions that the tough stuff lies behind us and everything else will be smooth sailing. We're climbing Speck Mountain, and before me is a sight I hadn't planned for—a sheer rock face. Running from the base of the cliff to the top is a long wooden ladder. To access the ladder, one must snag a rung with a foot while carrying a backpack on your back. If you miss the rung, you slip off and plummet to some terrible finality.

I stare at this scene in utter disbelief. Even though I have already faced death-defying danger on this trip—and was even warned by a physician in Carlisle, Pennsylvania, that I could drop dead hiking—this is the moment when it hits the hardest that I could actually die on the Appalachian Trail. If my foot misses the ladder, there isn't a thing to break my fall of at least two hundred feet. No one told me when I began this trek that you risk not only limb, but life hiking a simple trail through the woods. But here it is in all its grimness. To tackle this trail, one has to be a glorified rock climber, acrobat, or, as the mayor of Unionville once called me, a lunatic.

I agree. This is sheer lunacy.

I safely cross the mountain in a sigh of relief, just as rain begins to fall. Thankfully the terrain to Grafton Notch doesn't seem too unreasonable. But we still have a ways to go to reach the shelter for the night and then the blessed relief of a hostel the following day where Paul Bunyan will celebrate his seventeenth birthday on September 1. I have often heard of hikers whose birthdays were celebrated mid-hike. I'm glad it looks as if we'll find a perfect haven to enjoy a good time. Just the final ascent and descent of Baldpate Mountain, and we can call it a day.

The mountain shouldn't be any harder than what we've already experienced. But every day on the Appalachian

Trail is a different day. Every day you're tested, not so much physically as you are mentally. We arrive on the mountain's summit to be met by a cold, windy, misty rain. The little baseball cap I wear when it rains does little to prevent precipitation from collecting on my eyeglasses. I'm getting chilled too, clad in skimpy shorts and a T-shirt. Fog rolls in. What makes the day plain miserable is the descent off the mountain on slick rock faces. We can hardly see. We're slipping and sliding, wondering if we'll slide off the mountain to certain doom. We're cold, wet, and miserable. Paul Bunyan is crying. I'm crying right along with him as I think of us enduring such misery on the eve of his birthday.

When we finally make it to the next shelter, we hurry to put on dry clothing and heat water for warm drinks. We nearly played with the fire of hypothermia once more. Now I need to make a decision. Spend a miserable night on the trail in the cold and rain, or hope beyond hope we can somehow contact the hostel for which we have reservations the following night and see if they will take us a day early.

The warm drinks work their magic, and we're feeling better, along with the expectation of finding a place of refuge on this birthday eve. At the top of the next summit I call the hostel. Yes, we can spend the night if we arrive at the road crossing by four o'clock for our pickup. We need to hike another four and a half miles to make the rendezvous, through wet, slippery terrain. But the tears are gone and determination is renewed. We make hasty tracks. The mountains don't seem as steep, the rain not so pesky, the weather not so miserable when one has their sights set on sanctuary. Yes, a roof, a bed, and the granddaddy of them all, food.

Food is the one thing all hikers talk about, dream about, live for. Yes, we live for the miles to tick away one at a time, drawing us ever closer to our goal. But food, glorious food, hot sausage and mustard, wow. Especially when you're on the move all day, your body barely has enough time to digest what goes into your stomach before it's gone to keep the muscles working and the heart pumping.

We've already had our escapades of little or no food on the trail. We've also had some good eats. But the food that awaits us at the hostel called The Cabin goes beyond description for dirty, smelly hikers who feel pretty hungry at that moment. We arrive at our pickup point and wait only five minutes when a motor home pulls up. It reminds me of the one I used to camp in with my family long ago—the kind that took me to Shenandoah where this dream to hike the Appalachian Trail first began. I feel quite nostalgic but also grateful when the gentleman, who calls himself Bear, says to make ourselves at home. I rest on a nice couch in the rear of the mini motor home as he drives to our home away from home for the next few days.

We arrive at a beautiful log home with the welcome mat out for weary hikers. I have no time to clean up as Bear says the food is on the table and to come as I am. I manage to wash my hands and face before heading to the dining room where I stop and stare. Such food displayed there I can't even begin to describe. There are stacks of juicy hamburgers in buns. Salads and a huge homemade squash casserole. I slip into my seat as the tears are slipping out of me. Tears of gratefulness. Of thanksgiving over the bounty before me when only a few hours ago, Paul Bunyan and I were struggling, crying, pleading for relief from slippery rocks, cold, achiness, and fear. To sit down to warm food and smiling faces, I feel as if I'm sitting at the banquet table in heaven. Maybe this is a taste of what awaits in our heavenly home after the toil of this life, beset with all its difficulties. A feast that goes beyond words.

I'm then shown to a glorious chamber in this log palace—my own room for the night while Paul Bunyan finds a place in the hiker bunkroom. I stretch out on a luxurious bed after a warm shower. I feel like it's my birthday even though it's Paul Bunyan's. "Honey" (the wife member of the Honey and Bear team) also gives us our mail drop, which consists of food for the next section of trail and birthday cards for Paul Bunyan. And yes, there's a package from my own honey containing a few gifts and Paul Bunyan's famous birthday button—the one he has worn for his birthday ever since he was little.

The next day is a zero for us, meaning we don't plan to go anywhere. I dry out gear, take in the beautiful homestead, and talk to Honey and Bear about their hiking experiences. I catch up on e-mails and my online trail journal, and lounge around. That night Honey and Bear have a surprise for Paul Bunyan. They've invited a family with a son close in age to come celebrate his birthday. Dinner is another wonderful meal of barbecued chicken, corn on the cob, and other goodies. Then they bring out the cake that Steve helped arrange, complete with party favors. We're all decked out in hats and blowing horns. It's a real party. Paul Bunyan blows out seventeen candles in Andover, Maine, on the Appalachian Trail. Not many teens can say they have done something like that.

J O S H U A

When you start a long hike on the trail, most say it's mental not physical. When I think back on my days on the trail, one day in particular stands out for me—the day I hiked Baldpate Mountain. Physically it isn't very difficult. Mentally, it's an agonizing challenge. Baldpate is a completely bald mountain with very few trees. It's one big slab of rock. On a good day, you'd be able to see beautiful views long into the Maine wilderness. But on that day rain, wind, and fog make for unpleasant hiking weather and also make that rock face an ice face. Hiking boots are designed for traction on normal ground. When you put them on slick, flat surfaces they become like ice skates. And then along with carrying a backpack, it causes pain. I remember going down that mountain thinking again for the fifteenth time, *What am I doing here; I'm gonna die; this trail's gonna kill me; why am I here?* It really helps having a hiking buddy on a trail who can calm me down and help me keep from going off this ice face called a mountain.

From that point on, everything takes a turn for the better. It goes from famine to feast. From cold to beautiful warm heat. From treacherous wind to comfy chairs. The Cabin Hostel becomes a heaven of sorts. Hot showers and massive amounts of food (I ate five hamburgers that first night) are just a few of the things I will always remember.

Sitting at this big oak table with people around me, getting ready to blow out the candles on my seventeenth birthday, I'm thinking, *What better way to grow a year older than to be accompanied by friends, family, and FOOD!*

CHAPTER SIXTEEN

THE FINAL FRONTIER

UPPER MAINE

"The reward of a thing well done is to have done it."

~ Ralph Waldo Emerson

I was told one day back in New Hampshire that once we reach the Bigelow section of the Appalachian Trail, we'll be home free. For me as a goal-oriented person who always needs a goal laid out before her, the Bigelow Range is next in line. To conquer them requires more hiking over steep terrain. Whatever happened to the picturesque rocky coastlines one normally associates with Maine? I can envision lobster on the dock, the black rocks of Acadia National Park, cold ocean waters, the outlet stores of Freeport. In the interior parts of the state exists a world of challenging mountains. We have already been through the tough Mahoosuc Range. We know firsthand what Maine can dish out. And the Bigelows prove no different except they draw us ever closer to the finish line.

Just south of Little Bigelow we come to a magical moment where we see the phrase "2,000 MILES" spelled out in small rocks. Here we pause to take pictures and reflect. We've come 2,000 miles of trail, over hill and dale, through rivers and meadows, railroad tracks and roads, rocks and snake dens, bridges and caves. The next day we are rewarded even further. To mark the momentous occasion, a fellow hiker and trail angel named Old Fhart (don't ask me why!) and his crew of happy helpers makes us breakfast sandwiches. They even cut slices from a huge chocolate chip cookie with the state names written in frosting, along with the immortal words—174 miles to go. Paul Bunyan does his part by eating up the state of Virginia. Me, I just eat. And thank another set of trail angels for making more happy memories for hikers.

We're also running into more and more northbound hikers eager as we are to finish this thing. Over fifteen gather at shelters like Pierce Pond where loons lull us to sleep at night. I haven't seen so many hikers in one place since our early days on the trail in Georgia and the Smoky Mountains. When I had to leave the trail because of my ankle injury back in July, a bubble of hikers caught up to us. Now we're all trekking north with the same determination to see this hike through to a victorious conclusion.

After Pierce Pond comes the most famous water crossing on the entire trail—the Kennebec River. A hiker once lost her life trying to cross this wide river. Since then the Appalachian Trail Conservancy pays for someone to take hikers across in a canoe. Greeting us at the shore that day is a man with an appropriate trail name. "Ferryman" stands ready to shuttle us in his canoe with a white blaze painted on the floor. I take numerous photos of Paul Bunyan making the famous crossing. I once imagined myself at this moment, experiencing the crossing of the famous Kennebec as hikers have of old. Like other dreams that have come to pass, these are not simple imaginations conjured from words I've read in someone else's book. These are my moments. I'm living an adventure once thought maddening but already changing our lives forever.

After the crossing, and with the skies promising rain, we elect to call it a day and hang out at the Northern Pines

Resort. It boasts nice amenities like a restaurant and motel-like rooms to relax. I never tire in finding a place of refuge from the trail when hard rain begins to fall. I use the time to consider the next few weeks. Not many miles remain. What is my strategy for this final week on the trail? Take it one day at a time, as I learned to do for over 2,000 miles. But soon it will be the last day of our hike. The last day I will lay out my bedding for the night. The last time I will pack up my backpack. The last meal I will eat over my small canister stove. I will arise one morning to find the journey is done.

The final trail town for northbound hikers is Monson, a favorite place for resupplying and resting before entering the Hundred Mile Wilderness. Trail signs point out that hikers should carry provisions enough for ten days through this portion of the trail. As seasoned hikers, we plan to hike the wilderness quicker than that. We also have a new deadline to meet. After talking to Steve, I learn that my father-in law is planning to pick us up on Tuesday, September 18 at Baxter State Park. That leaves us six days to finish the hike, including climbing the final peak of Katahdin. Many twenty-plus-mile days will be our lot from here on in.

I venture to the post office in Monson, eager to see what Steve has sent in our mail drop for this grand finale. Enter post office. Exit without a box. I'm in a state of full-blown panic. I need that drop as it contains my medicine for the rest of the hike, besides food and other supplies. I run to the payphone and call Steve. Somehow (and don't ask me how) Steve called the post office ahead of time to discover that our package failed to arrive. He then express mailed me my medicine to arrive the following day. You must admit, his forethought is miraculous. The food we still need to purchase at the little old country store in town, but the medicine arrives in time.

If there's a beatitude I've come to learn on this journey, it's the *blessed are the flexible* one. I head to the itsy bitsy store to load up on noodles, toaster pastries, potato mixes, all the stuff I know gives limited nutritional value. But there's nothing else we can do. I'm glad at least for the excellent meals we have at Shaw's Boardinghouse where we're staying. I'm going to need every bit of protein and vitamins with the high trail miles we intend to do.

Now we're ready for the final stretch. We head on out and reach Little Wilson Stream that is hardly a stream. With the rain we've had, it's swollen to a river nearly thigh deep. It's another Maine quirk one has to get used to, like the massive mountain climbs, the sinking bog bridges, and yes, fording "stream" crossings that are essentially rivers.

In the coming days I start developing something new—pains in strange places. I've had aches and pains for months now, but this is different. I feel bones protruding in weird places in my hips, my back, my shoulders, my sides. I've never felt my bones like this before. I realize what's happening. I'm rapidly losing weight with the high miles and poor nutrition. Fat and muscle are melting off me. So far on this trip I've managed to maintain the same weight. Once I had the initial weight loss during the first eight weeks, the weight remained fairly steady, thanks to good nutrition. But with the last drop box missing, coupled with limited food choices of any nutritional value, the weight is slipping away, as is our dwindling food supply. At one point in the hike, Paul Bunyan and I stop for lunch in the midst of a twenty-plus-mile day. I pull out our remaining food which consists of a half box of raisins, one piece of jerky, a small hunk of cheese, and one saltine. It looks pitiful. There isn't much we can do but press on to the next resupply point at the grocery store at Abol Bridge.

To help cope with the pain and hunger in those final days, we're treated to our first grand view of our destination, the mountain we have hiked so many miles to see. Katahdin. It stands in all its majesty, growing ever larger as we hike north. One of the best views of the mountain is from Abol Bridge, where I take a picture. Katahdin looks perfect, and I feel perfect, too (if just a tad skinny). We're nearing the end. I can see it, taste it, yet it still feels a bit unreal to me. But right now, it's full speed ahead to the grocery store where we fill aching bellies with cheap hamburgers and stock up with tons of junk food we actually never end up eating.

I enter Baxter State Park, home to Katahdin, in a rather mind-numbing state. It's hard to put it into words. When one has dreamt a dream for so long, to see the end coming, you think it can't really be happening. But it is. I've hiked all the way here, several thousand miles. By this time tomorrow, it will all be over.

The next few miles introduce us to the park, including challenging stream crossings. But I make these final hurdles and approach Katahdin Stream Campground in eagerness to sign in at the ranger station. I savor each moment and each act as if they are sacred in some way. I'm so close to the end of this maddening dream of mine. Tomorrow I ascend the final mountain of the journey. Just ten miles of the Appalachian Trail remain.

We arrive at the Birches, a backpacker's campground for those seeking to ascend the mighty Katahdin the following day. There I meet an older couple we once ran into back in Virginia. They had suffered several medical setbacks including Lyme disease and a devastating fall, but they want so badly to climb Katahdin. The mountain is like the patriarchal grandfather of the trail. I admire their fortitude and wish them well. Climbing Katahdin is no easy feat. With an elevation over 5,000 feet, it's the most challenging ascent and descent of the entire trail. There's bouldering to master and steep terrain, among other things. But at the summit awaits a treasure—the infamous sign marking the northern terminus of the Appalachian Trail.

The next morning I'm up early to pack my gear for the

last time. I stuff my sleeping bag in its sack. I take the air out of my mattress. I gather up the rest of my gear that will be stored at the ranger station as we'll only carry daypacks for this final leg of the journey. Yes, this is my last day of hiking. My last day on the trail.

But miracles continue, even on this final day. It all serves as reminders that God has guided us to this point, watching over each and every step through weather and injury and doubt and good times, through starvation and friends and trail angels and everything in between. We begin our ascent on a cloudless day. One could not ask for better weather. The trail reminds me of the times we had back in New Hampshire—a steep trail with streams running through, coupled with rocks. It isn't until we get above tree line that the rocks really manifest themselves. I look out over the wide expanse open behind me. We're basking in scenic glory when a hiker lumbers up behind us. I recall seeing him last night at the campground, but we really don't know each other. Yet he comes forward, carrying a small black case.

"Hey, is this your camera? I found it down the trail."

I stare in disbelief and turn to search my little side pouch to find that my camera is indeed missing. Somehow it had dropped out without me knowing it. Without that camera, not only would I have lost all the pictures of our time in Maine, I wouldn't have any way to immortalize our final day. The magnitude of this nearly sweeps me over the ledge where I stand. I thank the hiker profusely but also see with my spiritual heart another miracle has come when I didn't know I needed it! But God knew how much this day means to us and to me. He is big enough to handle the big problems of the world and yes, the small problems like a camera lost on a mountainside.

We come to the boulder area on Katahdin's shoulder that requires one to negotiate hand and footholds on rungs embedded in the rock. We then enter what is called the tableland—a large flat area covered in tiny red bushes and fine gravely soil. Ahead of us yields another rise. I wonder if that is Baxter Peak, the northern terminus of the Appalachian Trail. I remain uncertain. But as we climb, I see a throng of people gathered at the top of the rise. This is it. The momentous end is drawing near.

I hand Paul Bunyan the camera and ask him to take some video footage of me making my final, emotional ascent. My feet are still swift, sure, and determined as they have been these many weeks. The sign grows ever nearer as other hikers watch my arrival. An outpouring of tears and thankfulness comes as I kneel before the weathered sign. I thank God for having brought me safely, 2,175 miles, to this final place.

The joy at a completion! Blissful and Paul Bunyan finish their northbound hike at Katahdin in Maine, the northern terminus of the Appalachian Trail.

I take some video of Paul Bunyan who places his hand reverently on the sign. I have no idea what is going through his mind at that moment. Only he can tell you.

JOSHUA

It is a nice day, a little bit chilly, but a good day to hike. Waking up that morning, looking up into the sky through the trees, knowing the mountain is here, I know this journey is coming to a close. Taking up my backpack for the last time seems more like closure than seeing that sign on Katahdin. I know my life over the last six months has changed. I'm not sure if I wanted it to. But I still have one more challenge ahead of me. The final mountain.

At first I want to carry my backpack up the mountain. After all, the pack is a part of me. Instead I decide to leave it at the ranger station, realizing things are definitely changing. Rock by rock, climb by climb, rung by rung we slowly hike the mountain. With my trail-hardened body accustomed to hiking, it doesn't seem that terrible a climb. Reaching the tableland and seeing the top of the mountain in front of us, the end gets closer. The final part proves quick and short. Reaching the summit, I see the famous sign on Katahdin.

What do I feel when I touched the sign? People like to ask that question. Honestly for me, not much. It isn't an emotional end but more of a tired end. All that day, I've been slowly realizing that this hike is coming to a close. By the time I get to the summit, it's more like, *okay, it's over.*

Now I know people say you're supposed to feel happy, sad, grateful, and joyful. Honestly it isn't till I took a video of my mother walking up to the sign and crying that it hits me what this all actually meant. Over 2,000 miles. A journey of great things but also injuries, broken boots, broken packs, mosquitoes, snakes, everything. Now the end has come. I get a tear in my eye just thinking about it all.

I turn then and look at the scenery southward from where I've come. I feel like I can actually see Springer Mountain in Georgia—the place where this journey started—and now Katahdin, where it ends.

LAURALEE

Yes, the journey is finished. I did it.

The End.

Or is it?

In the back of my mind I wonder. There is a time of letdown after you've accomplished a major goal in life. The questions follow. What's next? Is there anything left to accomplish? Where do I go from here?

PART II

SOUTHBOUND FROM MAINE TO GEORGIA
2008 - 2011

Chapter Seventeen

Madness Part II
Carry Me Back to Ol' Virginny

"What lies behind us and what lies before us are tiny
matters compared to what lies within us."

~ Ralph Waldo Emerson

Why would a person ever contemplate doing another
long-distance hike? Or the Appalachian Trail for that matter?
In all honestly, tucked in the back of my mind is the idea to
one day hike the trail again. Completing it not only from
Georgia to Maine but from Maine to Georgia. To be one of
the few women, if not the only woman in my age group, to
hike it in both directions. A lofty goal, and one I didn't really
believe I would do so soon after the first go-around. There
is my writing career, after all. House and husband, even as
Paul Bunyan has moved on to different waters.

At first I plan to hike the trail in small sections. Chipping
away the entire trail by hiking two scheduled trips a year.
Besides, a southbound venture is a far different beast than
my previous experience. I'm older and don't understand
the need to pace myself. The terrain is tough, especially for
those who begin in Maine. (Though I am initially working

on Virginia.) For the first time I'll be carrying all my own gear. No splitting up the tent, food, and cookware. It will all be carried by me, every last ounce. Ounces rapidly add up to pounds which can then equate to sore, aching muscles and blisters. I no longer possess a body conditioned by the rigors of the trail when I go hiking for only a week at a time. Every time I venture out, I'll return to square one—that is, enduring the aches and pains, blisters and fatigue, under the guise of a seasonal hiker. I will grow to appreciate what sectioners go through in their long, slow quest to accomplish the trail. Why it is they go out year after year, hiking with the intent to one day finish the entire Appalachian Trail. Whether it's over the course of a few years or fifteen, they are true trail warriors.

I forge ahead with plans to hike my native state of Virginia and get a taste of the trail in the opposite direction. I begin as I began for the 2007 journey, hiking the section closest to my back doorstep in Shenandoah National Park. I do it with a friend I met online. "Mercy" and her dog, also called Mercy. They are a unique team. Mercy the dog is a trained service animal. In her own right, Mercy the hiker was a park ranger and a Floridian. I've never backpacked with a dog that sometimes gets in the way of my trekking poles in her eagerness to lead the pack. But despite the windy weather and chilly rain, for which living close by has its advantages in seeking shelter, Mercy and I successfully hike the park and have fun getting to know each other.

I then do some hiking farther south with Signage. Spring has sprung, and once more I experience the pain of a tried and true sectioner. We have a good time reminiscing about our northward trek and the friends we met along the way. Steve even comes out to join us and fashions a wonderful Easter dinner trailside, complete with crab cakes and fresh asparagus. I'm enjoying the fall and spring schedule of hiking. I'll continue hiking the trail southbound in bits and pieces, taking the time to smell the roses and be with other hikers. It's all good.

I continue taking seasonal treks, but many times now as a solo hiker, without friends or family along for the journey. I have to figure out my own schedule, my own gear, what food I need to take, the safety issues. I learn a great deal in a week-long, solo backpacking trip. Am I preparing myself for some future long-distance solo trek yet to come?

I begin thinking about a month-long hike heading south. It's similar to when I began planning for the northern trek, but with some major differences. When my husband develops health issues, I think what better way to help the body recover than a long-distance hike. I recall the weight both Paul Bunyan and I shed over the course of our hike in 2007. (His final weight loss was fifty pounds and mine was thirty!) We never felt better. So Steve and I talk about going out for a month of hiking in Maine. I figure if I can get the tough stuff out of the way—like the notorious climbs in Maine's Mahoosuc Range, Mahoosuc Notch filled with house-sized boulders, followed by the unpredictable White Mountains of New Hampshire—it would set me up nicely to complete a southbound journey when the timing is right. And Steve gets the added bonuses of trekking along with me instead of staying at home, along with the health benefits.

We look at the summer of 2011 for a possible six-week extended hike. But life has a way of changing one's plans when there are changes of fortune. The year before I find myself inexplicably without writing work. A book contract I thought would materialize falls through. My calendar has opened up before me. Dare we try to move up our start date to hike Maine in 2010? It looks likely. I decide then to try and finish Virginia in the spring to prepare myself for a longer haul that summer. I've already done a fair chunk of my native state, but new goals are being realized. I'm not sure where it will take me or how long I'll be out this summer, but I plan to get ready just in case.

With my gear assembled and a spirit brimming in hope, I head out to pick up where I left off, with plans to hike the rest of my home state. Not two days into the hike, I suffer a knee strain after hiking too many miles and carrying too much pack weight. I return home to ice it and locate an adequate knee brace. One can be struck down, but the real thing is, have you been knocked out? I never believe I'm done for on a trip when injury rears its ugly head and tries to rob me of a goal. Nor do I feel this incident has put a crimp in my plans. I'm in this game to win, even if I still have things to learn, as the setback with my knee teaches me. I don't know everything there is to know about hiking and its many pitfalls on an ever-aging body, even if I have done a 2,000-mile hike in the past. For a fact, I can't do what the younger ones can. Or do the kind of hike I did a few years ago. The speed. The endurance, with older limbs not so easily adaptable to changing conditions and new stresses.

I must embrace a new mindset. *If this is your new goal, this Maine to Georgia trek, you're going to have to take it easy. You can't duplicate a 2007 venture after three years have passed.* This is a new game. Not GaMe as in Georgia to Maine. But a MeGa game. Maine to Georgia. And a game one must play to win.

I head out once more on my Virginia trek with the determination to limit mileage, weight, and enjoy some splendid spring scenery. I see things I never saw on my '07 trek, like the grandeur of the Keffer Oak in Virginia—the second largest oak tree on the entire trail. Heading north, I was too busy looking at the stile I had to climb rather than the grand tree nestled beside it. But hiking south, where they rerouted the trail through a different type of fencing, the tree stands in full array as I descend the grassy knoll. I marvel at it, take pictures, and realize how thankful I am for the opportunity to appreciate a thing of beauty that I missed on the first go-around.

At that moment, I realize this is going to be a different hike than 2007. A hike of better appreciation, not only of the scenery I missed but also the human spirit that goes beyond the call of duty. I am embarking on a new adventure, a new wander to see and learn even more. The previous journey has passed away. A new one is coming into focus.

Because of the setback with my knee, I fall short in completing the state of Virginia. I did head to northern Virginia to complete the trail from Harper's Ferry to the beginning of Shenandoah National Park where Mercy, her dog, and I began our trek the previous fall. With the trail in my native state 90% complete, I turn my sights to Maine when I will begin at the mighty Katahdin, the northern terminus of the Appalachian Trail, on July 1, to hike back to Virginia.

It sounds fine in my mind.

I hope it works out fine, too.

CHAPTER EIGHTEEN

MOUNTAINS AND MIRACLES REVISITED

MAINE AND NEW HAMPSHIRE

"Do not anticipate trouble or worry about what may never happen. Keep in the sunlight."

~ Benjamin Franklin

Three years have passed since my northbound success on the Appalachian Trail. Since then the knees are giving me more complaints. I've had multiple ankle injuries. Sometimes nerve issues creep up in my back. But still there's this overwhelming desire to do all that I can with the time given to me. To see all there is to see. To continue accomplishing goals and entertaining dreams. I wonder, too, if I have it in me to do another long-distance hike for months on end. If my husband would dare go along with it. If I can work it out with book editors. What will my friends think of me taking off again for an extended period of time?

So here I am, back to square one, pondering a southbound journey. This time I decide to take the hike a day at a time. No grandiose ideas or lofty goals. I plan to do this second attempt in increments. I'll hike the Maine portion with Steve this summer. If things go okay in Maine, I'll continue on to Hanover, on the border of Vermont and New Hampshire, and

156

so on down the trail. I'm also looking to see if this is what I'm supposed to do. It's not so clear-cut this time around. Once Steve leaves, for the most part I'll be hiking alone, carrying my gear, working out the issues and situations that are bound to pop up. It's a whole different ballgame requiring different planning and a different set of rules. But I still have a vision to complete the trail from Maine to Georgia. I'll see what happens and just go with the flow.

Steve and I depart for Maine and the doorstep of the mighty Katahdin where just three years ago, I was jubilant at finishing my trail adventure. Now I'm heading on another adventure, this time southward-bound. The contrast between the two will be quite startling, I'm sure.

For starters, we decide to take a different approach up Katahdin, using the Abol Slide Trail rather than hiking roundtrip on the Appalachian Trail. I've secured reservations for a campsite before and after our summit climb. We contact an old hiker friend from the past who lives in Maine. Mailar goes back to the very beginning of our trail experience when my son first received his trail name. He was one of several thru hikers we met on our hikes long ago in Shenandoah National Park. Now he generously offers to take us to our starting point at Baxter State Park and even plans to help us in the remote area of the Hundred Mile Wilderness where resupply is few and far between.

Little do I realize but Mailar will be the first in a long line of trail angels I meet on my southbound journey. These angels go over and beyond the call of duty to help a hiker in need. They will be my inspiration—a testimony of how they love others more than themselves. What a great lesson to learn on a hike which, for the most part, is a selfish activity. It's a life lesson I carry with me to this day.

Steve and I begin the assault of Katahdin on the Abol Slide Trail. It is just as the name suggests—a huge, rock-filled slide. We hike toward Baxter Peak into an ominous cloud enshrouding the mountain's summit. That cloud pours forth its vengeance as if to test our will and strength to go round two on this trail. We emerge above tree line facing forty-mile-per-hour winds and sleet pellets that lash at our unprotected skin. Fog hangs over the summit where only a few years ago, I rejoiced with my son at the journey's end set in spectacular sunlight. Now the journey's beginning has a black cloud hanging over it. At the summit, the clouds part for a brief time to allow for some views, which gives me some reassurance. We meet other southbound, would-be hikers looking to begin their grand 2,000-mile adventure. In contrast, there are a few northbound hikers rejoicing at their journey's conclusion. Quite a comparison between the hardened hikers completing the venture versus the batch of newbies just starting out.

Blissful back at Katahdin to begin her southbound quest.

That day we take ten whole hours to climb up and down the mountain. On my trek to finish back in 2007, we did the trip in six. I know better than to compare two hikes, or rather two different beasts. This is a beast all its own. I can still use what I learned from my previous jaunt, but a southbound hike has its own identity with its own mental and physical challenges, as I will soon find out.

We now fall into the business of day-to-day hiking, accompanied by a band of merry hikers that number about fifteen. We bump into one another during the course of a day or at shelters that night. There are the newlyweds who'd only been married a month before undertaking this six-month hike. (How's that for a perpetual honeymoon?) There are the Arizona guys who carry fishing equipment, knives, and even a pistol to do some real hunting and fishing trailside. At one shelter I come across one of the Arizona guys who has just nailed a squirrel with his pistol and is promptly dressing it, much to my chagrin. I must say I never experienced anything like that in 2007. Also among the group heading south are three other guys, a young teen couple fresh out of high school, a dad and his college-aged son. We are all from different backgrounds and norms of society, but the trail knits the unlikeliest of people together. We would never be friends in any other way in life. The Appalachian Trail has that power to make strangers into friends, to create community where there is none, to encourage one to help another in times of need.

Our trail angel Mailar, who took us to the doorstep of Katahdin, now goes even further in a call of service by offering to slackpack us the fifteen miles over the Chairback Range. On this day I'm hiking with all the young people as the oldest one in the bunch. On a particularly steep section of rock, I begin to clamber up it when my foot suddenly slips. I'm surely going down but for one of the Arizona guys who grabs my hand and pulls me to safety. Whatever the trail delivers, hikers look out for one another. We are comrades in arms. We are a small but close-knit community.

The day proves long and hard as we crawl those fifteen

miles to where Mailar and Steve are waiting for us. (Steve took the day off the trail to nurse some nasty blisters.) What was supposed to be an eight-hour trek took us twelve. Oh, the joy of going southbound. But we are rewarded that night with a late steak dinner and the comfort of real beds at Mailar's childhood home.

We hike on the following day, and after our first big rest day in the town of Monson (where Steve earns his trail name Papa Bliss after arranging with Mailar to deliver a surprise watermelon to one of the young hikers in our company), our group of fifteen begins to drift apart. We are hiking different mile days as we head south toward the bigger mountain ranges arrayed before us. We are never a solid group again after that, but to this day we remain in contact with one another.

Papa Bliss and I continue through Maine over increasingly difficult and steep terrain. At one point on the trail, it seems like I could walk right off the mountain's summit and plummet to the valley below. I take careful steps and manage to make my battered knees hold out. There are techniques I have learned to preserve such things as my aging knees. Patience is a virtue in steep, rocky terrain. But eventually things do catch up. A hiking pole breaks. Feet are hurting. We grow weary and decide once we cross the Saddleback Range of southern Maine to leave the trail for a week. Papa Bliss needs some time to heal. I need new hiking poles, and my family needs assistance. My mother just returned from a fateful trip out west where she had fractured her hip in a fall, and I plan to go to their home and help them settle.

But even good plans can have challenges. My parents have a difficult time readjusting after the injury. At their home, while I'm helping Mom into the car, her wheelchair escapes down the driveway. I dash after it and in doing so, promptly strain my left hip. With the injury, I decide to stay off the trail a few more days, so we take the extra time to head to my in-laws' for a visit. For some reason tensions run high. My mood sours.

When Papa Bliss drives me back to Maine at the end of the week (he is returning to Virginia and work), there's a difference. I recall past partings in tears. Not this time. I sense this is a journey of contemplating my future, of wondering why I'm here on this earth and what I'm supposed to do. My return to the trail is a testing of waters. I will be alone on the most difficult sections. I'll have plenty of time to consider life in all that I endure. It will be a thorough self-examination.

The trail does not disappoint in the area of hardship and the need for endurance. A few nights later I'm huddled in my tent during severe thunderstorms that dump five inches of rain. I'm up most of the night drying off the tent with the only towel I have—a pair of underwear. The next morning the Appalachian Trail is a raging creek. I give up trying to keep my feet dry and just slog through the deep water. But I have a place of refuge at The Cabin where Paul Bunyan celebrated his birthday back in 2007. Honey and Bear greet me with open arms and give me a private room. I take the opportunity to regroup and prepare before I enter the notorious Mahoosuc Range and Mahoosuc Notch. It's been tough so far, but I'm still hiking, with grit and determination.

When I enter the Mahoosucs, I'm feeling pretty good mentally. I'm getting my trail legs—that is, my physical stamina is improving. I've figured out how to handle steep terrain without sacrificing life and knees on steep rocks. It's looking and feeling good. When I arrive at Speck Pond Shelter, I meet up with another southbound hiker and her dog. She plans to hike through Mahoosuc Notch that day, the notorious mile filled with huge house-sized boulders. Originally I planned to stop short of the notch, but with the good time I'm making, coupled with a hiking buddy to boot, I decide to go for it.

We enter the notch and encounter the huge boulder field. She teaches me a little technique that I'd not done on earlier hikes—dropping your pack down from above so you can negotiate the steep rock face unhindered. Things are going well.

That is, until the hiker's dog—immature and untrained—refuses to follow her through the maze of boulders. He runs and hides among the rocks. On top of that, rain starts to fall. We're now in a major dilemma. The girl calls in earnest for her dog but to no avail. I wonder what to do as she plans to go back over the boulders and search for the dog. I look at the nasty rocks we've just traversed and realize I simply can't go back over them again. Reluctantly I tell her I'm going on and hope she can soon catch up. But as I hike, I hear her crying for the dog and I shudder, wondering if I have made a terrible mistake by not staying behind. All I can do is pray for her situation and mine.

Huge rocks like massive houses hem me in. The going is treacherous. Rain continues falling in earnest. At one point I lose my way in the boulder field and literally end up in a deep hole made of rock with no way out except up. I wonder if I'll end up dead in this place. My pack is so heavy, fully loaded from a resupply at the hostel earlier that day. I have to hoist some thirty pounds up and over my head before I can climb out of the hole. Somehow there is the strength to do it as I haul myself out of the pit. But each step proves more painful than the last. The notch is like some evil entity seeking to imprison me in a stony tomb. What a difference from 2007.

At last I stumble out of the place and cry in relief. My legs are so bloody and bruised, I look like I've been in some immense battle (which I have, in a way). There's miles left to the shelter over more steep terrain, but at least this nightmare is over. I'm shaken by the encounter, but I keep on hiking and arrive to find the shelter area packed and every tent platform occupied. I am completely spent, hungry, in pain, near the end of myself, and there is no place to rest my head. What else can happen?

But then I hear an angelic voice break through the barricade of mental and physical anguish. "Hey, if you don't mind, you can share our tent platform with us and set up your tent here."

I look around. Two girls already have their gear and tarp set up, but they dismantle it to make room for me and my tent. Like sweet oil, I welcome the kindness of strangers. I'm so spent emotionally and physically, I can barely move. I thank them profusely and take their picture to remember my hiker angels.

Then I hear more voices; the girl with her dog and another hiker have arrived safely. They were able to locate the dog, to my relief. But too exhausted to even talk to them let alone cook, I consume an energy bar for dinner; one of the few times I don't make an evening meal. I crawl into my sleeping bag, nearly crying myself to sleep from the sheer relief of having survived this day. Here's to a better tomorrow.

After a few more days of hiking, I arrive in New Hampshire. It's been a tough go of it, but somehow I've survived, and now I look forward to resting in Gorham. After the experience of Mahoosuc Notch, I realize that despite my perceived setbacks, I do possess a will to survive whatever the trail gives me (though it does its best to rob me of everything). I know there are more tests to come, but thankfully I never know just when or how they will come, and that's probably better.

The White Mountain Region of New Hampshire now lies before me, but minus the paralyzing fear I had on my 2007 hike. After all, I have already dealt with fear and tough terrain big time in Mahoosuc Notch. The Whites have to be better than being lost in a maze of stone fifteen feet high. Two miles down the trail, I'm walking along a narrow bog bridge that traverses a swampy area. Trail maintainers use these narrow boards to protect tender vegetation or protect the hiker from swampy messes. The boards this day are slick with rain from the previous night and covered by a layer of moss. Suddenly my foot slips right out from underneath me. I land backward on the bog bridge, directly on my tailbone. The pain is excruciating. I literally cannot move for a few moments. I know I've done something huge, maybe even fractured something.

Oh, no! Oh, God! Here we go again.

I struggle to stand, but the pain is intense. Somehow I manage to make it to my destination for the night, Imp Shelter, but I'm uncertain what to do. I recall the incident back in '07 with the calf injury when I had to get off the trail. Back then it was easy with transportation close by. Way up here in New England, it's not so simple. Home is twelve hours away. I know if I leave the trail, it will be for good. The hike will end here and now.

I set up inside the shelter for the night, doubtful of my future. It's a sickening feeling. When the caretaker for the shelter area comes by to collect the fee for the night, I consider telling him about my injury. But I don't. Another hiker strolls in, an older man out for a few days. We share a little about our hike. I suddenly launch in, telling him about the fall I suffered earlier that day and how I worry this is the end of my southbound attempt.

"Do you mind me asking your symptoms?" he asks. "You see, I'm a doctor. So tell me what happened and what you're feeling."

I stare incredulously but tell him everything, especially my concern that I may have broken my tailbone. Meanwhile I'm still reeling over the fact the one lone hiker who came in tonight is a physician, of all things!

He nods. "Honestly, even if you did break it, there's nothing that can be done. You can hike on it, but it will hurt like crazy. Just take a lot of ibuprofen."

I'm speechless. Here I am, in the middle of the Whites,

having suffered what I thought was a devastating injury that would take me off the trail. The doctor/hiker eases any misgivings about continuing the hike. Whereas other physicians long ago tried to give me a ticket of doom and gloom (like the doctors back in 2007 over my supposed heart ailment), his is a ticket to hike on.

But challenges still remain. The next morning I discover that some rodent has chewed a nice fat hole in the drinking tube to my water system. So my hydration system is useless until I can get a new one. For the next day's hike I have only a small bottle to carry water. I hike, coping with the pain from my tailbone injury and limited water supply, until I reach the first of the AMC huts called Carter Notch.

In 2007 this was not the friendliest place. I recall my son and me dealing with the head guy at the hut who did not like thru hikers. But the gal this afternoon welcomes me with enthusiasm. She finds me a spare water bottle, serves me food, and even writes me a note guaranteeing a work-for-stay option at the next hut where I can do some tasks in exchange for a meal and sleeping on the floor. Wow. I am a witness to blessing in the most fascinating way.

At Pinkham Notch, I plan to shower off the grime, soothe my aching tailbone, and retrieve my mail drop before heading into the always unpredictable Presidential Range. It's kind of strange as last time I trekked through here I was with my son and just survived a terrible bout of the stomach flu. This time I arrive as a solo hiker, experiencing this all on my own, the good as well as the bad. I obtain a rather cold shower and proceed to pack up my food from the mail drop when a woman comes walking into the gear room. She introduces herself and asks if I'd like a place to spend the night at her home in North Conway. She'll even feed me.

I stare in disbelief. Then I hear she had also hiked the trail back in 2007, the same year as my son and me. I find an instant kinship with M&M. She drives me to her condo near North Conway and promptly offers a feast of lobster and white wine, better than the finest restaurant. I'm totally amazed and blessed. Here I am, a lone hiker, dining on a four-star meal, safe in a nice house and with great company, in a place where I can rest, ice my injured back, and spend a quiet night. It's humbling in ways I never expected.

I feel ready now to take on the Presidential Range, well nourished by M&M and armed with my note from the gal at the last hut so I'll have a place to stay that night. I tackle the trail above the tree line, enjoying beauty beyond description and good weather for the traverse. At the huts I wash dishes in exchange for a great evening meal and a spot on the dining room floor. I come out of the Whites not entirely unscathed but still walking south.

Blissful in one of the most scenic stretches in the White Mountains of New Hampshire, the Franconia Ridge

Should we worry about what we will wear? What will we eat? Where we will stay? A water hose with a bite taken out of it? A potentially broken tailbone? If God Himself cares for the sparrows, won't He also care for us, oh ye of little faith? It's a lesson I need to grasp along the journey of life, and I'm starting to see the light.

CHAPTER NINETEEN

SOLO SOUTHWARD IN THIRST

VERMONT TO NEW JERSEY

"I'm in my prime. There's no goal too far,
no mountain too high."

~ Wilma Rudolph

With most of the difficult trail in Maine and New Hampshire now behind me, I'm feeling pretty good about the hike. Hikers trying to tackle the whole Appalachian Trail are told that 90% of the work lies in the tough terrain of those two states. I have mastered all the peaks, along with injury and weariness, rain and sun, isolation and friends. The only thing left as I head south is miles and days. So I pick up some speed, enjoying, for the first time, the lack of steep terrain and the need for rock climbing skills. I feel like I'm in my prime now that I have accomplished most of the battle. The only goal left is crossing the finish line, still many months away.

In a matter of days, I start feeling a nagging sensation in my left calf. Back in 2007, such pain in my calf forced me off the trail for a week. I realize that in my exuberance to hike at a quicker pace, my legs aren't accustomed to the speed. Most likely I've strained a muscle. If there isn't a real mountain to climb on a hike, there's always a physical mountain by way of an injury. I did overcome the tailbone injury in the Whites. Now I have a strained calf to add to it.

I immediately go into action, wrapping the affected extremity with an elastic bandage and stretching the muscle as much as I can. I also cut my mileage to let it rest. In time, and with prayers that Steve whispers over the cell calls I make, the leg slowly adapts. I've learned I don't need to rush the hike but can take it one step at a time. Isn't that like our walk in life when we try to rush? Sometimes if we go ahead of the plan, we end up getting hurt. A steady, sure pace is best. Not too slow. Not too fast. Just right. The Three Bears of conquering a trail.

Speaking of bears, I've seen little in the way of wildlife so far on my trip. Until southern Vermont when I hear branches breaking close by me. I pause and look to my right, wondering what on earth could be making such a racket. Suddenly I come face to face with Mrs. Moose dining on green leaves in the thick woods. I chuckle. I always imagined seeing moose in Maine and New Hampshire, but I never thought I would in southern Vermont. I never know what lies around the bend.

Vermont is a beautiful state, made even more beautiful by the fact that this time my shoes are not coming off my feet in thick mud, typical of hiking in this state. The trail is bone dry. Little rain has fallen in New England over the summer months. Locating safe and reliable water sources is an issue I rarely dealt with in my previous wanderings. Now I find myself relying more and more on my trail maps for water sources and using what I call "hiker intelligence." The hiker communication grapevine is alive and well in matters having to do with the trail. I listen carefully to what hikers say about water conditions, especially as Vermont is known for streams originating from beaver ponds.

In Massachusetts the water situation becomes increasingly

difficult. In one section alone, nearly all the sources are dry. I stop and inquire of a hiker who painstakingly describes to me one source in a stretch of twenty miles that I need to locate for my evening water. A hiker requires water not only to cook dinner but to have a supply ready for the next day's wander until another source becomes available. He tells me where to find it, but I wonder if I can. It's like trying to locate treasure by way of a verbal treasure map in the wilderness. I look over my options on a real map, but all the streams are outlets flowing from beaver ponds. It appears the only reliable water source is the one described by the hiker.

I trudge ahead, hoping to find it. Miles pass. I realize the shelter area where I will spend the night isn't too far distant. Without water it will be a most unpleasant evening. At last I come to a dry streambed that flows downstream to a beaver pond. The inlet is dry but for one large puddle of water. Taking out my small cup, I gingerly scoop up water into my bag, thinking how much we take for granted this life-giving liquid flowing freely out of faucets at home. That is, until faced with the lack of this resource in the woods. The puddle is the only water I've found all day, but it's enough to see me through the night and on to the next source. There are third-world nations in which water is a precious commodity. People devote themselves to raising money for wells in these countries. I have a better appreciation and understanding for water's life-giving value. It truly is liquid gold.

The search for liquid gold continues as I head into New York, where again it's bone dry. One day I lug the equivalent of six pounds of water over eight miles to my destination that night. I find myself toting extra water frequently, which adds to the hike's difficulty. But what can you do? Better to have the water (and suffer the pain of carrying it, along with the griping) than not to have it and go thirsty.

In New Jersey I nearly meet my match in the water situation. The day is particularly warm, and the water sources few and far between. I think of Moses, wondering if I can strike a particular rock with my hiking pole and have water gush out and fill my dry throat and empty water bottles. I pass a Scout troop on a break while on my way to one water source. I arrive to find the stream bone dry, and my water bag is close to empty. I head back to the main trail, wondering what I'm going to do. I meet up with the scoutmaster of the troop I just saw at the trail junction. He asks how things are going. I admit to him I'm nearly out of water and there's none anywhere.

"Well here, have some of mine!" He offers me a liter from his own supply.

I accept it with grateful thanks. I didn't need to strike a rock with my pole. I was supplied water in other ways, through the kindness of others.

Unfortunately the liter of water he gave me doesn't last long as temperatures soar into the 80s. Again I find myself nearly out of water as I trudge up a hill. I feel like Hagar of old, thinking I might as well die of thirst out here. I meet hikers heading downhill, and they ask the proverbial question: "How are things going?"

"Terrible," I answer plain and simple. "There's no water."

"Well, I'm stopping at the next road crossing," one of the hikers says. "I don't need my water." He then produces a liter and a half of liquid gold, which I again accept with grateful thanks. Only this time as the hikers continue on their way, tears fill my eyes. Once more, my silent request to God's ears is heard through the mercy of hikers on my path, giving me plenty of water to see me through.

But the story doesn't end here. I discover later the hiker who gave me his water is being picked up by a gal who was once a hiker herself. And that female hiker remembered my name from attending a picnic the previous year, hosted by Steve and me for hikers in the mountains of Virginia. Seeing my comment on my trail journal, the hiker recalled with fondness the picnic and the food that helped her on her trek. We gave her food in Virginia and in turn, her friend, via some obscure meeting on the trail in New York, gave me water. Amazing when one considers the probability of such an encounter. How can one say there are only mere coincidences in life?

The kindness of fellow hikers and townspeople continues to follow me as I hike south. Yes, I am hiking solo, but really there is nothing solo about this venture. God is with me. He opens doors for contacts with those whose acts of kindness go beyond words. For example, I'm trudging south through Connecticut when I run into the newlywed couple I met long ago in Maine. They are full of stories of people who helped them along the way, giving them food, shelter, rides, etc. I think back to the time several weeks ago in New Hampshire with M&M who cooked me a lobster feast. I have so much to be thankful for, yet I still harbor some jealousy over their good fortune. I tell God, *It's great they are being taken care of on the trail. Do I fit in the plan of care anymore? Or was that it for me?* Yes, it's pure selfishness to even ask such a thing. But I say it in all honesty after having one's flesh beaten to a pulp on a long drawn-out hike. Soon it's pushed aside for the trail laid before me. After all, I agreed to put myself out here. I don't deserve help, nor do I really need it. Or so I think.

A few days later I check my e-mail and find a note. It comes from a couple who live near the New Jersey state line. They say their hellos and then to my astonishment, offer me a place to stay if I want it. I stare at the invitation in disbelief. Here I was bemoaning my condition while jealously watching others receive multiple invites. Suddenly out of nowhere comes this offer. I sheepishly agree. And instantly I am humbled.

When I arrive at the couple's home some time later, they go over and beyond what I could ever ask or think in the angel department. They feed me, allow me to use the washer for my nasty clothing, even give me a day of slackpacking. I carry a daypack for a tough, rocky section straddling New York and New Jersey.

During this stay I also receive the unexpected news from my agent of a writing lead. Remember, the writing area of my life had been quite dead. Now a publisher wants me to write a novella, and I need an idea for it *right now*. Okay. I'm out hiking a trail. I have no access to previous files for my fiction works or even a computer. But it just so happens that I'm staying with this generous couple who now offer me the use of their computer. I look at the couple and the surroundings I find myself in, and the idea for a story comes naturally. I base it on an inn that takes in weary travelers and gives a downtrodden stranger hope. Thanks to my wonderful hosts, the idea is gratefully accepted. Who says one wanders by feet only? I guess that little wandering of the heart is not in vain but a catalyst to a story idea I hope is meaningful to others.

But now I need to submit a full proposal of the idea in order for the editor to accept and contract it. This leads me to reconsider my hike at this point. I must admit I miss home in Virginia and my husband. I miss decorating for the autumn season, picking apples, drinking fresh-pressed apple cider. When I reach the Pennsylvania border, I decide to return home for a week to work on a synopsis for the story idea and do some things on the home front.

But there is a price to pay. Because of the delay, I will not be able to complete the entire trail southbound this year. I must leave Pennsylvania and Maryland until next spring.

Yes, a man plans his way but God directs the steps. My plans are changing course, but there is peace. When the journey continues, it will be at the right time and the right conclusion for the right season of life.

CHAPTER TWENTY

SOUTHERN HOSPITALITY, TRAIL-STYLE

SOUTHERN VIRGINIA TO GEORGIA

"You are the only person on earth
who can use your ability."

~ Zig Ziglar

What are your abilities in life? Have you ever considered them? I suppose I can put down two roles at which I excel—writer and hiker. My husband would love to add wife to the list of credentials, as he's most glad to have me home for a week. The house is in dire need of some maintenance, and I enjoy decorating it for the autumn season. I complete the proposal for the novella, and my editor contracts it to come out next Christmas. But completing the southbound hike remains my primary focus. I'm in good shape right now, having hiked from Maine to Delaware Water Gap in Pennsylvania. I would do well to at least complete the trail from where I left off in southern Virginia and hike to the southern terminus at Springer Mountain, Georgia. That will leave Pennsylvania and Maryland until next year, ending in Harper's Ferry. And Harper's Ferry is a fine place to finish—a nostalgic town nestled beside two great rivers and home to the Appalachian Trail Conservancy. Surely they wouldn't mind a hiker celebrating another milestone at their front doorstep.

I convince Steve to drive me to southern Virginia, where I will wander another few weeks to Springer Mountain in Georgia. I can't say he's thrilled by the prospect, but he's been my support and encourager. Without him, none of this would be happening. He recognizes my dreams and desires. So even if it is with reluctance, he bids me farewell, and I head out.

Autumn is in full swing as I wander south. The vibrant colors of the season come forth in the mountains and dust the trail with newly fallen leaves. At least the acorns aren't such an issue as they were up in New England. There they act as tiny missiles from above and coat the trail like marbles, sending one into a fateful skid if you aren't careful.

Autumn also brings new faces to the trail in the form of hunters. Wearing orange or at least carrying something of orange is a necessity. I soon see why when I round a bend in the trail to find a hunter poised with a rifle in hand, aiming into a nearby meadow. Some have their hunting dogs with them. The yelping and barking can be heard for miles. Other hunters merely stand around on the trail with their walkie-talkies as if hoping something will happen.

All this makes for a slightly unsettling time as a solo female hiker. With this, safety comes to mind. I recall only one time back in New Jersey when I thought I was being followed. When I picked up the pace, the stranger did too. It made me nervous. I wondered what to do. Then I looked to my left and saw a stone wall in the woods. I made a mad dash for it, as quick as one can do carrying a full backpack. I got down behind the wall and waited. I heard a cough. I waited another fifteen minutes before emerging to continue on my trek. I never saw him again. The moral of the story is: exercise caution. Most would say a woman is crazy to hike alone. But as a Christian, I believe I'm never alone. If I meet others on the trail who inquire if I'm hiking alone, I deny it.

I believe Someone greater than myself is always with me, in every situation, as my miraculous adventures have shown. So when I meet a bunch of ragtag hunters on the trail with hound dogs in tow, I recall His protection and guidance. I walk in confidence, but I still take necessary precautions. I don't camp near roads. I have my whistle handy. Most importantly, I listen to God-given intuition. If something doesn't feel right, I don't hang around.

I also listen to warnings given by others. Once a couple warned me of a strange hiker lurking around the next shelter, in the very area I planned to camp. He'd made threatening gestures to the other hikers and might have been looking for drug money. I heeded the warning and went farther than I ever thought I would, over twenty miles to avoid the area, and camp in a nondescript place off trail. I believe trail angels exist in many forms, including those who warn of danger.

Trekking southward in the fall, any hikers I do come in contact with are few and far between. Many nights I'm alone at a shelter or campsite. I don't mind it much because of the many trail miles I'm putting in. I barely have time to set up camp, get water, cook and eat before bedtime at 7:30. When one treks hard miles, the body needs rest, sometimes ten hours or more to recuperate. I would lie in my tent, listening to inspirational music and think about things. You do a lot of thinking when you hike. You consider your life, where you're going, what the future holds. I think, too, of the story I want to write when I return, the upcoming holiday season (for which I'll be glad to be off trail to celebrate). I never feel lonely, to be honest. The mind can be a great occupier.

Most of all, I enjoy meeting people. When I begin receiving invitations to visit fellow hikers and families along my route, I eagerly accept their hospitality. Those visits become the highlight of my time on the trail as a southbounder. It is vastly different than when I hiked north with Paul Bunyan. I stay as a humble guest in people's homes, learning about them, sharing our common interest of the trail. One hiker in Erwin, Tennessee called 10K treats me to lunch. We enjoy food and talk trail talk. As I progress south through the Great Smoky Mountains and on into Georgia, I gain another invite from a couple—the parents of the newlyweds Steve and I met in Maine. They invite me to their home in Georgia. I learn of their great love for plants and animals while I enjoy a wonderful, home-cooked meal. They awake before dawn the following morning to take me back to the trail. Talk about loving your neighbor as yourself. Or rather loving the hiker!

Crossing the state line in the Great Smoky Mountains National Park.

My final contact, only a few days shy of the end, is from fellow hiker Winkle and her husband. Winkle, short for Rip van Winkle, is interested in a long-distance hike herself, as are the friends she's invited for dinner. I have a good time sharing hiking stories over another great meal. But I also think about my final days of the hike this year and how it will end at Springer Mountain, the southern terminus of the Appalachian Trail. What a difference from that day long ago in 2007 when I began a northbound quest and the nice group we had enjoying the summit of Springer Mountain. This time there will be no such companionship. No fanfare or hoopla. It will only be me.

For the first time on the hike, I feel alone.

I pack up my gear anyway to spend my last days out on the trail for the year. The final day on Springer will culminate several months of hiking, and what a time it has been. Unfortunately the weather this day is nasty, with a cold, wet rain that chills me to the bone. Huddling at a shelter to eat some snacks, this is not a great way to end my southbound venture, alone and wet on Springer with no one to take my picture by the big sign embedded on solid rock. I'll likely have to stay a miserable night in a shelter, too. But isn't that the essence of trail life? You take the good and the not-so-good. I pray about it, but there isn't much else to do except shoulder my backpack and head for the end.

I hike with as much determination as I can muster on a rainy day, thinking about my many adventures. Suddenly I spot two hikers coming in the opposite direction. I recognize the smile beneath the rain hood. Then I hear my name. It's none other than Winkle and one of her hiking friends I met at dinner a few nights ago. I stare in surprise, wondering what on earth they are doing out in this kind of weather.

"We thought we'd come hike the summit with you," Winkle says. "And since I knew you wouldn't have anyone to take your picture, we can do that, too."

Wow! Even at the end of the journey, in rainy weather, cold and wet, God heard the feeble-minded yearning of some woman out on a muddy trail and found her companionship atop the southern terminus of the Appalachian Trail! We have a good time hiking that last mile. At the summit they take the revered pictures. Winkle then invites me to spend another night in her warm home instead of staying in a cold shelter.

Blissful with trail angel Winkle who surprised her with a hike and a photo opportunity at the southern terminus at Springer Mountain, Georgia.

What a glorious conclusion to this hiking season of my life, by way of unexpected blessings given by trail angels. The men and women I have met along the way, both north and south, truly made my hike and epitomized the essence of loving your neighbor as yourself. They were Good Samaritans of a special kind.

The next day Steve arrives from Virginia to drive me home. I still have two states left to complete the Appalachian Trail southbound, but I have good memories of the time I spent in the wilderness this year. I take time to marvel at faithfulness in physical areas as well as the heart, in wanderings, in contemplations, in my writing, in my walking. Even the summit of a cold, wet, dreary mountain was made warm and inviting like a summer day by those who went out of their way to keep a lonely hiker company. These are the kinds of experiences that draw me back to the trail even to this day.

In trying to shelter our lives, sometimes we try to control it. It becomes difficult to see and hear what we need to.

But out in the middle of the woods, vulnerable and utterly dependent, the whispers of God are heard in clear fashion. It is evident in every facet of our being, through every answered prayer no matter how strange that prayer may be and at every challenge we meet.

I arrive home in time to celebrate Steve's birthday, our wedding anniversary, and the upcoming holiday season. But the final segment of the trail to complete my southbound trek is not far from my thoughts. Pennsylvania and Maryland are still to come.

CHAPTER TWENTY-ONE

NO WIND NOR STORM NOR FLOOD...

*PENNSYLVANIA TO
HARPER'S FERRY, WEST VIRGINIA
2011*

"If you can dream it, you can do it. "

~ Walt Disney

Nothing is more beautiful than springtime in Virginia. The azaleas, redbuds, and dogwood are out in colorful array. Daffodils and tulips burst forth from the ground. Birds sing and build nests for their young. And the Appalachian Trail calls once more. Some say it's Springer fever—that malady that strikes a hiker with an unmistakable urge to be at Springer Mountain and the start of another hiking adventure. For me it's more like a fever, Pennsylvania-style. I'm ready to embark on yet another hike, but a sense of accomplishment is waiting in the wings. I've walked north from Georgia to Maine. Now I've walked from Maine to the Pennsylvania/ New Jersey border and from West Virginia to Georgia. All that remains is Pennsylvania and Maryland—250 miles or a little over two weeks of trail time—before I see another goal realized. A second completion of the entire Appalachian

Trail. Steve also plans to join me for a week. Sharing this experience with others makes it all the more meaningful. I discovered how wonderful it was to have others share your experiences after the two hikers met me on Springer Mountain that raw, rainy, foggy day last November. I want Steve to be a part of this adventure as he was in the beginning and will be when I hike into Harper's Ferry on that final day.

Now plans fall into place for the final leg to the finish line. Through a hiker website called White Blaze, Steve and I link up with a generous trail angel and hiker Ernman who agrees to shuttle us to our starting point at Delaware Water Gap. On top of that, he also offers us the use of an apartment for the beginning stretch of the hike.

When we arrive, Ernman rolls out the welcome wagon, volunteering to shuttle so we can do some slackpacking of a twelve-mile stretch. It makes for an easier time, especially when the rains come in earnest. At night I'm back in a nice, comfy apartment where I can grab a shower and dry out. It's true heaven.

Pennsylvania is definitely having its rainy season this spring. We battle unpredictable weather ranging from sun to fog to downpours. On the descent into Palmerton over the rocks of Lehigh Gap, I worry about hiking down slippery boulders, recalling my ordeal back in 2007 while trying to get up those same obstacles. But having done the tough terrain of northern New Hampshire and the Mahoosuc Range of Maine, the rocks are nothing to fret over. In no time we've mastered them and are hiking up the other side of the gap.

I also recall the famous Pennsylvania rocks scattered along the landscape from my previous venture through this state. Miles and miles of knobby rocks ready to trip you up and do a number on your psyche as well as your feet. I've learned over my many miles of hiking to take the trail as it is comes, one step at a time. I'm able to negotiate the terrain with minimal difficulty and find myself enjoying the trip much more than in 2007. There is something to be said about knowing what awaits you. And realizing what the mental battle is all about. The trail can mature your way of thinking. Make you steadier, surer, confident. It changes you. You become a veteran of the trail.

The rocks of Pennsylvania greet Blissful in her last two states before completing her southbound hike.

Even though I'm okay with the hike, Steve is not having a good time. Unbeknownst to me, his back pain is flaring up. He's had an ongoing issue with a herniated disk and finds it difficult walking for any distance without crippling pain. Our pace slacks off when we stop frequently and wait for Steve's pain to diminish. I realize this is not working out for him or for me. I encourage him to have our trail angel Ernman pick him up at the next road crossing and take him back to our car parked at Wallace Gap. I will then hike on and meet up with him later. While I do at times enjoy a wander on my own, I'm disappointed Steve has to end his hike so soon. It's tough when your spouse cannot enjoy the wonders, being sidetracked by pain.

Later that day I meet up with him, and we find a place to spend Easter weekend. We welcome the day with remembering the Resurrection in the Bible and then enjoying brunch at a quaint Pennsylvania Dutch restaurant down the road. It serves all the favorites, including German sausages and slices of shoofly pie. A bit of happiness in an otherwise disappointing time for Steve. Now he must depart for home, and I'll be on my own for roughly ten days of hiking. There's a certain emptiness found when one's life partner leaves. I feel it whenever Steve drops me off at a trailhead. We are team players in a game, and when one isn't there, it makes the journey a bit more uncertain. But I know he is with me in spirit. Praying for me. Keeping me in his thoughts and close to his heart as I walk this walk.

Now I turn my thoughts to God's heart on what to do. Should I go this way? Should I do that? God promises to guide us at all times. We can cast our cares on Him, for He cares for us. For example, I arrive early to a shelter area and try to decide whether to press on to my intended destination for the night. The skies are overcast with a promise of rain in the forecast. I make the decision that if it starts to rain, I'll call it a day and stay at the shelter. I arrive at the place to gather water and sure enough, a misty rain starts falling. I'm disappointed, but a bargain is a bargain. I stay and set up inside the shelter where a very opinionated northbound hiker is already in residence.

The next day when I arrive at the campsite where I'd originally planned to tent, I find it completely inundated with water and mud from the storm. It would have been a most unpleasant and wet night had I elected to continue on and stay here. So it does well even in the midst of the woods to stop and listen, even if you are in doubt. You are better for it.

The weather continues to show itself a mighty force on the trek south. Pennsylvania has had its share of rain as I slog through woods that look more like swamps. I detour around them as best I can but find the trail challenging. It's amazing how the hike changes from year to year or even season to season. Sometimes it's so dry that one can't find water anywhere, like what I experienced in New England. Other times you receive so much if it, the trail becomes a brook in need of fording.

Arriving just shy of Duncannon bordering the Susquehanna River, I set up shop in the Peters Mountain Shelter for the night. It's a solidly built, two-level structure, and I'm glad for it as the skies darken in an angry spectacle. The wind picks up, foretelling a stormy night to come. Another hiker is in residence, and she's decided to tent. There are times that a tent in harsh weather isn't always the best option. I fear this is going to be one of those nights. In fact when the wind gusts, I hasten over to her tent and inquire if she might want to spend the night in the safety of the shelter. She declines. I find myself the lone occupant of this vast, two-story shelter, watching the wind and rain and storm clouds swirling around in a spiral-like fashion indicative of tornadic action. I huddle in the back of the shelter to wait out the storm, all the while saying a quick prayer for the hiker in her tent. It proves a ferocious wind-driven, rain-soaked night.

The next day I pack up, none the worse for the rough night. But a mere half mile down the trail, I find a huge tree had just fallen across the trail. I wonder then what would have happened if a tree like that had fallen on the shelter! Later I learn there had been a wave of tornadoes that swept across the east, wreaking destruction, including a devastating tornado in southwest Virginia.

But the dark skies above remind me of the power still left in the departing storm. A sudden burst of heavy rain soaks me to my skin. I see other evidences of the storm in the rising water levels of the Susquehanna River. The rushing water is but a few feet below the main bridge carrying cars across the river. Tires, logs, and other debris are being swept away in the fierce current. A campground is under water, and even parts of Duncannon experience flooding. It's all rather surreal to me. But once inside the old Doyle Hotel in town where I enjoy a burger and some rest, I'm thankful for a safe place out of the ravages of the elements.

Security can be fleeting, though, when I again face the aftermath of a storm in the form of high water throughout the Cumberland Valley, the next section in Pennsylvania. I traipse through muddy, cow-pie laden fields, waterlogged from the copious rainfall. Soggy and muddy shoes on my feet are the mainstay these days, even if it's bright and sunny. Still I make progress despite the swampy, muddy trail and rain showers that greet me every other day.

I've seen few hikers out and about, and for the most part, I've been on my own. But then I receive a greeting of a different sort at a town park in southern Pennsylvania. I'm hiking along, minding my own business, and suddenly happen upon fourteen loose dogs, led by two inattentive owners. The dogs pounce, and suddenly I feel a strange sensation on my right leg. One of the smallest dogs has actually taken a bite out of me. I'm bleeding.

I can't believe it. After nearly 4,000 miles of trail, surviving snow, storm and hail, an injured tailbone, slippery rocks, a sprained ankle, I suffer my first dog bite of the trip. Incredible. I thought I had seen it all. But one never knows what lies in wait.

Now the end is nearing. I cross the Mason Dixon line that ushers in the final state of Maryland on another cold and rainy day. The clouds eventually give way, and pleasant, sunny weather greets my final days hiking into the town of Harper's Ferry, West Virginia. Here I will finish my southbound hike of the Appalachian Trail. There will be no fanfare, I know. No one to say, "Good job!" But I'm thankful I can do this, that the old body is still able to move after 4,000 miles to recognize another goal. It's still a good feeling to accomplish another awesome feat and at my age. Most of all, I'm thankful for the memories and the people I've met along the way.

I close in on Harper's Ferry—made famous by the John Brown raid, Civil War history, as well as home to the Appalachian Trail Conservancy. Here I plan to stop, have my picture taken, and officially enter my name as completing a southbound hike of the trail.

Steve drives up from Virginia to meet me near the C&O Towpath, where we enjoy an easy four-mile river walk to the historic town. While I hike, I don't think much about what is actually happening. My mind is blank. I thought I might have some nostalgic wave wash over me, completing yet another full hike of 2,000 miles, but I don't. It's rather odd. Maybe it's shock.

Steve jumps ahead to take some video of me as I take my final walk across the bridge spanning the Potomac River.

Oh the joy of completing a southbound hike of the Appalachian Trail in Harper's Ferry, West Virginia to become a 4,000 miler!

The end has arrived. At the trail sign in the town of Harper's Ferry, I kneel in a prayer of thanks and then stand, raise my hands high, and give a loud cheer. It's hard to believe I've finished the trail for a second time.

Little do I realize that my finish has also garnered some attention. Two women leading a class of young people now bustle over. "Have you just finished the trail?" one asks.

I give them an enthusiastic "Yes!" They congratulate me, which adds to the moment. I take my time with Steve as we trace the winding trail through town and then on to the Appalachian Trail Conservancy to record my completed hike and have my picture taken.

Suddenly I'm greeted by the eager staff who welcomes my accomplishment with open arms, congratulations, and announces that I'm the first official completion for 2011. With that they break open the sparkling bubbly for me and pour glasses, all the while snapping photos outside the center as I toast the trail and my hubby. Here I thought there would be no kudos at the end of this trek. Shame on me! I have never felt so blessed by such camaraderie and celebration. I guess one can say this is the final act of trail angel mercy on an adventure that has spanned the years. And what a way to finish!

A long way to walk. Four thousand miles. Or rather 4,356 to be exact. How are we able to accomplish something that goes beyond what we can think or do? Caught up in a situation, you have no choice but to persevere and go forward. You might look back, shake your head, and wonder, *Did I really do that?* From one end to the other and back again? Through the pain, the rain, the hurt, the hunger, the terrain? But through beautiful but challenging scenery, provisions bestowed in times of need, the hikers and trail angels met, the memories cherished.

I can't help but feel grateful for every mountain climbed where the beauty of a view waits. Every maddening thought that can make the impossible possible. Every miracle found in nature and in nature's man.

This experience has become a place of strength for me. A place I can tap into when I find myself in circumstances of needing to trust. To look beyond my own strength to the miraculous. To see the love of others that beckons me to love in return. To see and cherish beauty beyond description. To be thankful for the small as well as the large. To fully realize my life scripture that has come to pass, not once but twice. That I can truly *do ALL things through Him who gives me strength.*

BOOK DISCUSSION QUESTIONS

1. Have you ever had a plan fall through? Or a plan that did not turn out the way you expected? How did it make you feel? How did you deal with it? How did it change you in the end?

2. Think back on a dream or goal you have made in your life. In what ways have you been encouraged to fulfill your dreams and goals? Who or what has helped you along the way? What Scriptures or life verses have encouraged you?

3. Have you ever thought of giving up when the going gets difficult? Think of one special person or persons who helped you when you needed it most. Describe what happened and what it meant in making it through your difficult time.

4. We are so blessed to live in a land of plenty that we sometimes take it for granted. What did this example of the author's situation that day at Overmountain Shelter teach you about thankfulness? Stop right now and be thankful for even the small things, like the meal you had today or the glass of water out of the faucet. Especially for the family and friends in your life. And think of ways perhaps you can reach out to others who have less.

5. What is your greatest fear? In what situation have you found that fear tested? How did you overcome that fear—or if you are still in the process of overcoming, what steps are you taking?

6. Think back to a time you were challenged to get along with someone who didn't have the same plans, dreams, or

goals as you. How did you react? How did you cope with the changes it brought in you?

7. Think of the times you've worried over something beyond your control. What did it do to you emotionally and physically? What did you do in the wake of these worries and what happened as a result?

8. Have you ever had instances of encountering angels unaware? Or found angels coming to help in your time of need? Recall your experiences and write them down or share them with others so when the going gets tough in this life, you can remember God's faithfulness.

9. Dwight D. Eisenhower once said, "Plans are nothing, planning is everything." Many times our plans fall short. Or they change. Or they are met with challenges. Think of an event in your life where you attempted to plan it out but found yourself taking a detour instead. How did it make you feel? What did you do to cope with it? What was the end result?

10. Take time to write down what this book has meant to you and what you have gleaned from the stories shared. I would be grateful if you drop me a line and let me know your thoughts. My e-mail is: blissfulhiking@gmail.com

ACKNOWLEDGMENTS

With heartfelt thanks to those who made this journey of 4,000 miles and the book possible:

My husband and partner in everything, Steve "Papa Bliss"

My son and hiking partner in '07, Joshua "Paul Bunyan"

The staff and editors of WhiteFire Publishing—Dina, Roseanna, and Wendy—with grateful thanks for taking a chance on this book

My parents: Robert H. and the late Lucille A.

My in-laws: Ken and Marie

My siblings: Rob, Deanne, and Andrea

Best friend Sherry

Grace Covenant Church of Charlottesville, Virginia

Laurie, Dave, and staff of the Appalachian Trail Conservancy

Rich and staff at Rockfish Gap Outfitters, Waynesboro, Virginia

Winton and staff of Mountain Crossings Outfitters in Georgia

The White Blaze Hiking Community

Editors, past and present, at Barbour Publishing

Tamela Hancock Murray

Friend Jackie

Neighbors Ross and Lisa and family

Trail Angel Mary Anne

The nurses and ER doctors at Carlisle Medical Center, Pennsylvania

The late Ed Garvey

The family from Pittsfield, Massachusetts

The Hills

The McCormacks

The Weber family

The Wheelers

Hiker Angels (by their trail name or other): 10K, 357

Magnum, Baltimore Jack, Beach Bum, Chef Boyardee, Circuit Rider, Cookerhiker, Disney, Dr. B, Warren Doyle, Emerald, Ernman, Flint, Frolicking She-Dino, Hikernutt and Tim, Honey and Bear, Leprechaun, Lone Wolf, Mailar and his wife, M&M, Mercy, Odyssa, Patrick, Ragamuffin and MeGaMo, Raindog, Sherlock, Signage, White Crow, Winkle and Greg, and the hikers, family and friends who offered their critique and feedback on this manuscript: Joshua, Sherry, Claudia, Shannon, Sue, and Vera.

Thanks be to God who truly does beyond what I could ask or think.

CPSIA information can be obtained at www.ICGtesting.com
Printed in the USA
BVOW00s1242301013

334993BV00001B/1/P